ADVANCED CARDIOVASCULAR LIFE SUPPORT (ACLS) PROVIDER MANUAL

A Comprehensive Guide Covering the Latest Guidelines

M. Mastenbjörk M.D.

S. Meloni M.D.

CONTENTS

FREE GIFT

GET ONE OF THESE EBOOKS FOR FREE:

Medical Reference Pamphlet
ACLS ebook
Pulmonology ebook
Neurology ebook
Mini Medical Dictionary

Scan the following QR code:

You will be redirected to our website.
Follow the instructions to claim your free gift.

UNIT I : INTRODUCTION TO ADVANCED CARDIAC LIFE SUPPORT

Cardiac arrest remains one of the most common causes of death, both in and out-of-hospital settings. Each day, many lives are saved because of the application of the principles of Advanced Cardiac Life Support (ACLS). ACLS represents a series of memorized steps which, when performed in sequence, can greatly improve survival rates of patients who have respiratory and/or cardiac arrest. These steps are based on the latest evidence available in literature, and are updated every few years; the most recent updates were made in 2020.

While Basic Life Support (BLS) can be studied and performed by all lay people, anybody who works in the medical field is encouraged to become certified in ACLS. ACLS training allows medical personnel to react to emergencies in a reflexive, quick, and coordinated manner. BLS does not require the use of advanced equipment or medication. In contrast, ACLS may require experience in the use of certain equipment and medication, and will require some basic medical skills. This does not mean that ACLS can only be provided within the hospital environment. When properly trained, ACLS providers may combine their skills with available equipment to provide life support at the site of arrest.

This handbook is designed for all medical professionals who undergo ACLS training. It aims to establish a sound understanding of the principles of ACLS, and the latest guidelines. The content in this handbook is in compliance with the 2020 guidelines recently released by the American Heart Association (AHA). All the protocols illustrated here are based on up-to-date evidence.

UNIT II : THE ACLS CHAIN OF SURVIVAL

Cardiac arrest is a life-threatening event that can have a high mortality rate unless high-quality intervention is immediately available. To maximize the chances of survival, the AHA has adopted the 'chain of survival' concept. The chain of survival is a series of actions that can decrease the mortality rate following cardiac arrest, provided it is initiated in the proper sequence, and executed correctly. Like any chain, the chain of survival is only as strong as its weakest link, and therefore, all steps in this chain are equally important.

ALGORITHM 1: CHAIN OF SURVIVAL OUT-OF-HOSPITAL AND IN-HOSPITAL

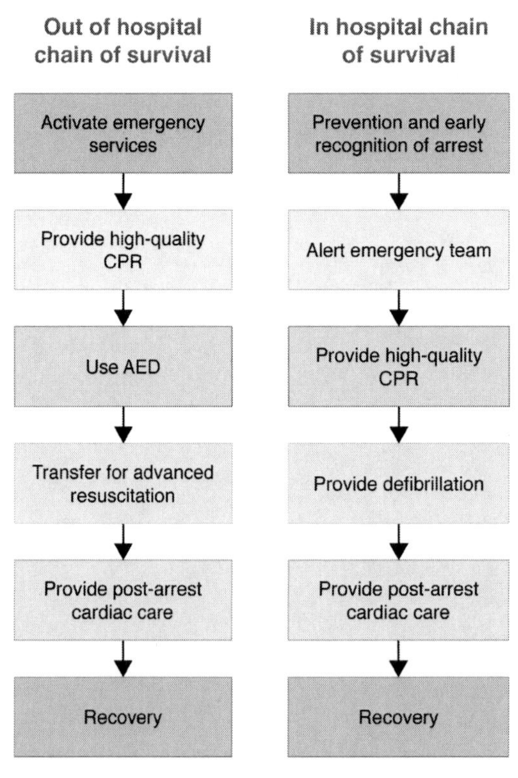

DECODING THE ACLS CHAIN:

The importance of each of the above links in the chain of survival is discussed in greater detail below:

Enable early recognition and access:

It is well recognized that early initiation of life support measures can increase survival after a cardiac emergency. For early initiation, two key initiatives are required – recognition, and alerting for necessary resources. In the out-of-hospital chain, a layperson may recognize that an emergency exists only when the patient collapses. The first thing to do in that scenario is to alert emergency services so that the patient can have access to more intensive life-saving resources as soon as possible. However, in the hospital setting, it is possible to recognize an impending emergency before it actually occurs. Therefore, the first step is prevention of arrest, and its early recognition. This step is targeted at both caregivers and nurses who may be monitoring the inpatient. The second step in the in-hospital chain of survival is to alert the emergency team. In a hospital, there are usually two categories of teams that respond to emergencies:

Rapid response team:

The goal of the rapid response team is to *prevent* the occurrence of respiratory or cardiac arrest. The rapid response team may be called when patient deterioration is noticed, for instance:

- Extreme bradycardia (< 40 bpm) or tachycardia (> 140 bpm)
- Bradypnea (< 8 breaths per minute) or tachypnea (> 28 breaths per minute)
- Hypertension or hypotension (> 180mmHg or < 90 mmHg of systolic pressure)
- Sudden deterioration in mental status
- Oxygen saturation < 90%

Code team:

More commonly called the 'code blue team', the goal of this team is to resuscitate the patient *after* respiratory or cardiac arrest has already occurred. Usually the code team is called if:

- Patient is unresponsive
- Patient stops breathing
- Patient has no pulse

Early initiation of CPR:

The efficacy of cardiopulmonary resuscitation is maximum if it is initiated immediately after collapse. Therefore, this step forms the second and third links respectively in the out-of-hospital and in-hospital chains of survival. However, the AHA estimates that less than 40% of patients who collapse receive layperson-initiated CPR. The 2020 AHA guidelines have placed greater emphasis on encouraging layperson-initiated CPR, as the risk of harm of CPR is far less than the benefits. CPR essentially consists of chest compressions in combination with rescue breathing. The ratio of compressions to rescue breaths is 30:2 for adults, irrespective of the number of rescuers. In children, the ratio is 30:2 if a single rescuer is present, and is 15:2 if two rescuers are present. A detailed description of the technique of CPR is given in the partner handbook on Basic Life Support.

Early defibrillation:

When cardiac arrest occurs, the heart basically fails to pump blood. This is often because there is an alteration of the electrical rhythm of the heart to such an extent that it fails to stimulate mechanical pumping action. Delivering electric current using a defibrillator can 'shock' the heart into regaining its normal rhythm. Defibrillation is effective when it is performed three to five minutes after arrest; after this the rhythm may cease altogether. Therefore, this is the next important link in the chain after CPR. Out of hospital, an automated external defibrillator (AED) is usually used, which can detect the kind of abnormal rhythm and deliver a shock if appropriate. In hospital, however, a manual defibrillator is used.

This will require the rescuer to analyze the rhythm and make the decision whether or not a shock is to be delivered.

Advanced cardiac resuscitation:

The difference in BLS and ACLS is defined by this step. Lay rescuers would, at this stage, ensure that the patient is transferred to a hospital for advanced care. However, advanced life support providers would, at this stage, begin more precise patient management. Advanced airway access may be obtained, if needed, and parenteral access is obtained to deliver drugs and fluids. A systematic assessment of the patient begins at this stage. These steps are discussed in the unit on ACLS survey.

In the hospital, response teams will usually consist of trained ACLS providers. For out-of-hospital arrests, the emergency response team must ideally consist of two providers trained in ACLS, and another two trained in BLS.

Post-cardiac arrest care:

While the previous links in the chain are targeted at saving the patient's life, this link emphasizes the need to preserve normal body function after return of spontaneous circulation. Proper post-cardiac arrest care focuses on maintaining optimum oxygen levels, and preserving proper heart and brain function.

Recovery:

In the 2020 guidelines issued by AHA, a sixth link, recovery, has been added. Recognizing that the aftermath of a near-death experience can be stressful, this link emphasizes the need to offer continued support to both patients and families. Such support must begin at the end of acute treatment and continue through multimodal rehabilitation process.

QUESTIONS

1. When should a code blue team be called in the hospital?
   a. Blood pressure falls below 90 mmHg
   b. Patient has no pulse
   c. Respiratory rate is more than 28 breaths per minute
   d. Oxygen saturation falls below 90%

2. What is the first link in the in-hospital chain of survival?
   a. Prevention of cardiac arrest
   b. Alert emergency team
   c. Start CPR
   d. Provide defibrillation

3. Which of the following links was added to the chain of survival in 2020?
   a. Prevention and early recognition of arrest
   b. Transfer for advanced resuscitation
   c. Post arrest cardiac care
   d. Recovery

UNIT III : ANATOMY AND PHYSIOLOGY OF THE HEART AND NORMAL ELECTROCARDIOGRAM

To properly understand how ACLS works, it is first essential to have a thorough working knowledge of the anatomy and physiology of the heart. The heart is basically a muscular organ, which is hollow inside. The hollow interior of the heart is separated by thick walls of tissue, or septa, into four chambers. The upper two chambers are referred to as atria, and the lower two are called ventricles. These four chambers collect blood and circulate it throughout the body.

The walls of the heart are made up of cardiac muscle. This muscle has two kinds of fibers. The first kind, lining the atria and ventricles, are normal fibers similar to skeletal muscle fibers, except that they have a longer duration of contraction. The second kind is special fibers which have poor contracting ability. However, they have excitatory and conductive properties, and can generate and conduct electrical signals. While the normal fibers contribute to the mechanical functioning of the heart, the special fibers contribute to its electrical activity.

Mechanical activity of the heart:

Contraction of the atrial and ventricular fibers results in a pumping action, which is responsible for circulation of blood. Only deoxygenated blood passes though the right heart, and only oxygenated blood passes through the left heart (Figure 1). The right atrium receives impure blood from rest of the body through the superior and inferior vena cava. It pumps blood into the right ventricle, which in turn pumps deoxygenated blood to the lungs through the pulmonary artery. The blood is oxygenated in the lungs, and sent back to the left atrium through the pulmonary vein. This oxygenated blood then enters the left ventricle, which pumps it to the rest of the body through the aorta.

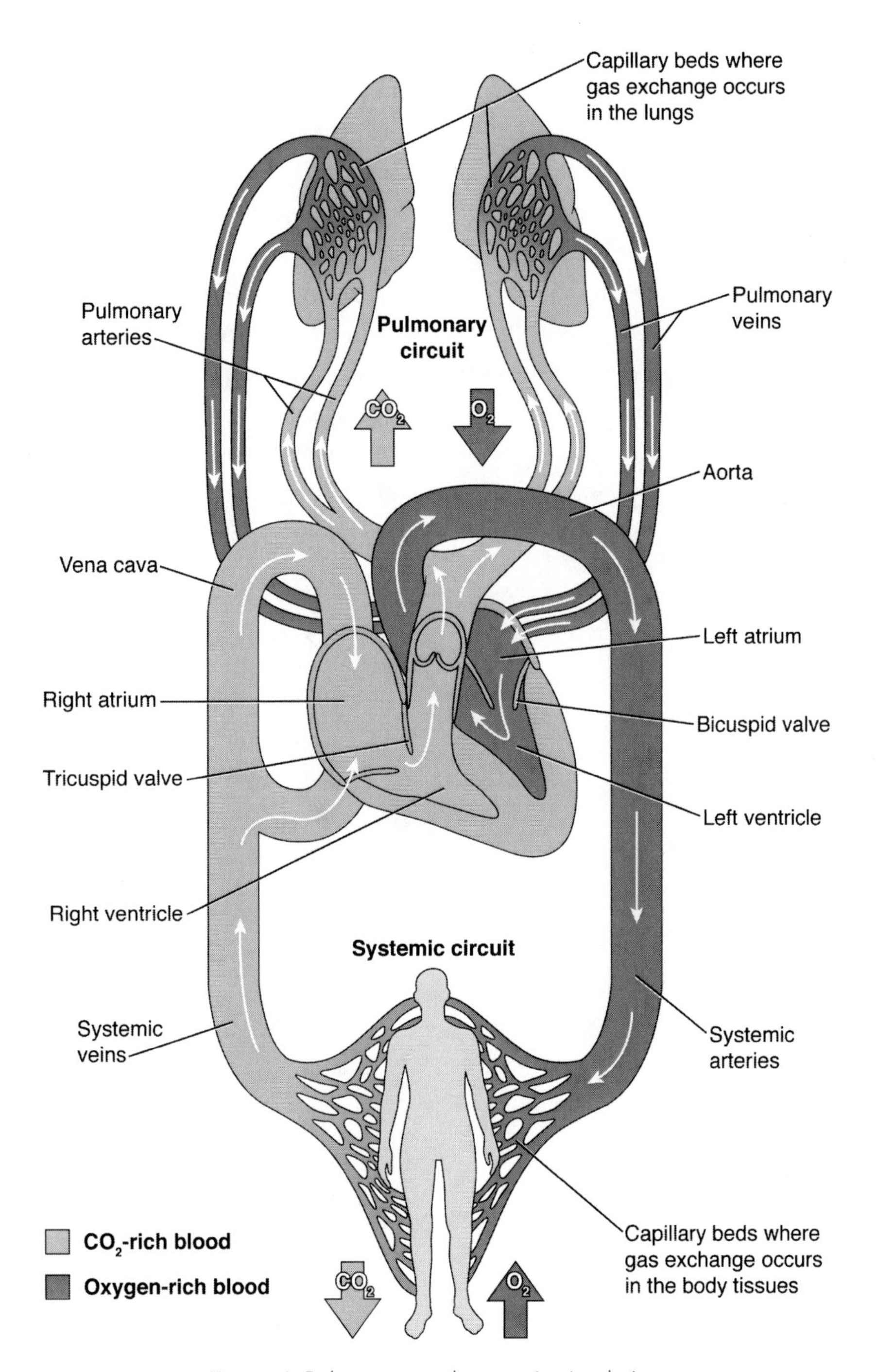

Figure 1. Pulmonary and systemic circulation

Electrical activity of the heart:

The mechanical pumping activity of the heart occurs in a specific rhythm, which is essentially regulated by the heart's electrical activity (Figure 2). The right atrium contains a mass of specialized tissue, called the sinoatrial (SA) node. This node generates electrical impulses at an average rate of 60 to 100 per minute. These impulses are conducted to both the right and left atria, causing them to contract. They also travel downwards through the special conducting fibers to another node, called the atrioventricular (AV) node, located at the bottom the right atrium. From here, the electric impulse goes into two conduction pathways, called the Bundle of His, which conduct the electric signal into the right and left ventricles, which in turn contract. When each cell of the heart is electrically stimulated, it goes into a phase of depolarization, followed by repolarization.

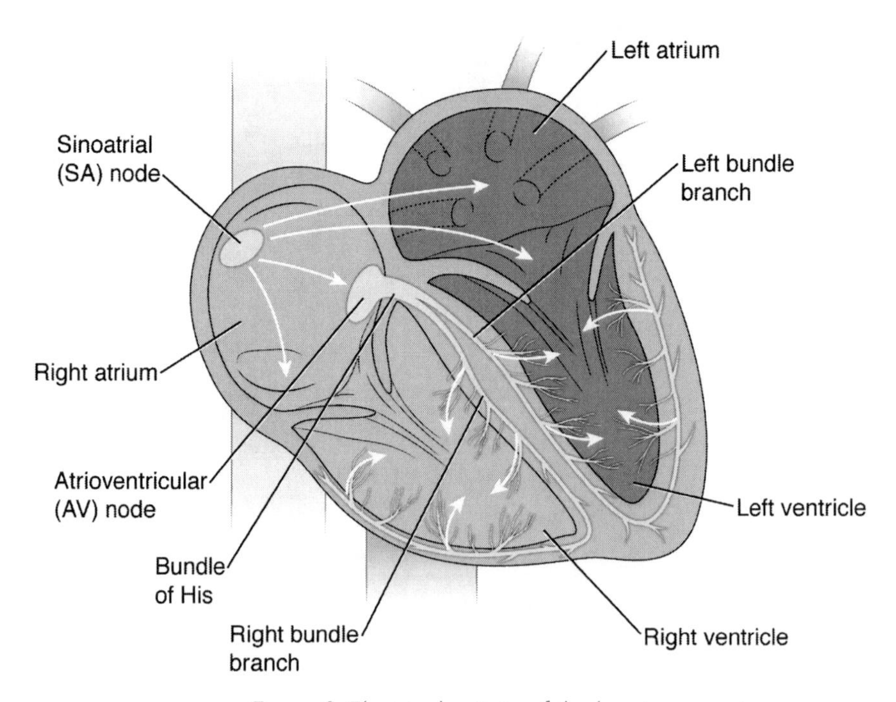

Figure 2. Electrical activity of the heart

Cardiac cycle and Electrocardiogram:

The activity that occurs in the heart during a single heartbeat is referred to as the 'cardiac cycle'. The cardiac cycle is divided into two phases:

- **Diastole:** During this period, the atria and ventricles are both relaxed. The atria receive blood from the vena cava and pulmonary veins, and the same flows passively into the ventricles. At the end of diastole, both the atria contract, propelling a further amount of blood into the ventricles.
- **Systole:** The right and left ventricles contract, pushing blood into the pulmonary artery and aorta respectively.

The electrocardiogram detects the electrical activity that occurs during each phase of a cardiac cycle, and records it on a strip of paper, or displays the output on a monitor. The standard ECG wave consists of three important components (Figure 3):

- **P wave:** This is a small wave which represents atrial depolarization.
- **QRS complex:** This is a larger and taller wave, which represents ventricular contraction and ventricular depolarization. Atrial repolarization also occurs during the QRS complex.
- **T wave:** This represents ventricular repolarization.

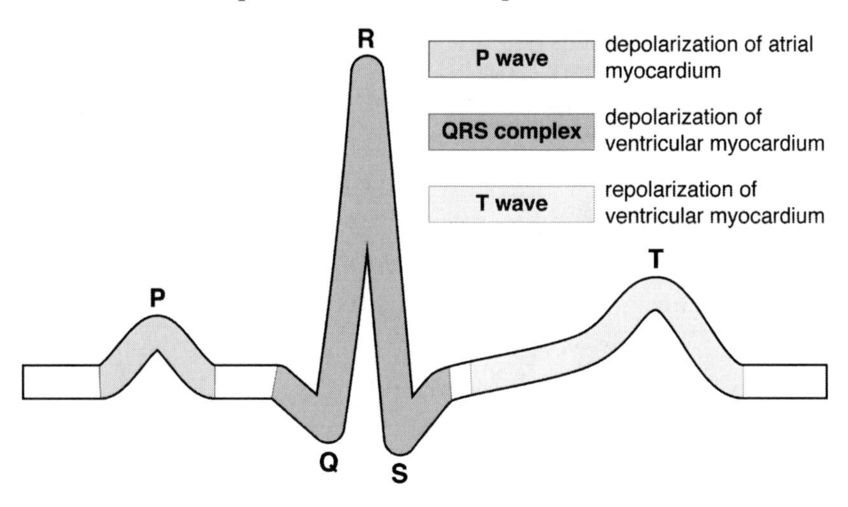

Figure 3. The normal ECG wave

If there is a cardiac emergency necessitating ACLS, the normal rate and rhythm of the heart may be altered. This can be viewed on the ECG monitor, or as a printout.

A normal ECG reading looks as follows:

Normal Sinus Rhythm

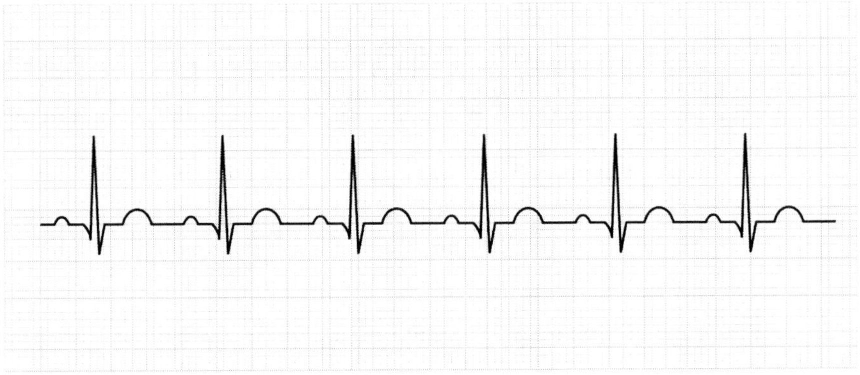

Figure 4. Normal ECG reading

Basic steps in ECG interpretation:

Comprehensive details of ECG interpretation are beyond the scope of this book. For an ACLS provider, it is essential to interpret only a few key details, which can be done at a quick glance. These include the following:

- Rhythm: Assess if the rhythm is regular or irregular. This is done by looking at the distance between successive 'R' peaks. In a regular rhythm, these distances would be approximately the same, while in an irregular rhythm, these would vary.
- Rate: Usually, the heart rate is automatically displayed on a cardiac monitor. If reading an ECG printout, look for identical points (such as the peak) on two consecutive P waves, and count the number of small squares between these points. Divide 1500 by the number of small squares to get the atrial rate (1500 small squares = 1 minute).

The same method, using points on R waves, gives an estimate of ventricular rate.

- P wave: Check if P waves are present or absent. If present, check if the waves have normal rounded shape, and whether they are upright. Also check if all P waves are similar in size and shape. All P waves should be followed by the QRS segment. If all these parameters are normal, there is no problem in initiation of impulses at the SA node.
- PR interval: Calculate the PR interval using the method described for rate calculation that is, using the number of squares between the P wave and R wave. The normal PR interval should be 0.12s to 0.2seconds. A prolonged PR interval may suggest some blockage in the AV node transmission.
- QRS complex: Successive QRS complexes should have the same size and shape, and should point in the same direction. Each QRS complex should be followed by a T wave. The QRS complex duration should be around 0.04 to 0.1 seconds. If a QRS complex is prolonged, it may indicate a bundle branch block.
- T wave: Check if T waves are present or absent. Sometimes T waves could be merged with P waves. If present, check if all T waves have the same size and shape, and whether they point in the same direction as the QRS complex. Also look at the status of the ST segment and QT interval. Normal QT interval should range from 0.36 to 0.44 seconds. T wave variations can have several causes:
    - T wave inversion – lack of oxygen to the heart
    - Peaked T wave – hyperkalemia
    - Flat T wave – hypokalemia
    - Raised ST segment – myocardial infarction
- Ectopic beats: If fibers outside the SA node stimulate the heart, it can result in ectopic beats, which will appear as irregularities on the ECG.

ACLS treatment usually depends on the kind of rate or rhythm alteration. Therefore, each of the above factors must be evaluated quickly and accurately during the ACLS survey. This is discussed in subsequent chapters.

QUESTIONS

1. Which blood vessel sends blood into the right atrium?

   a. Aorta
   b. Pulmonary artery
   c. Pulmonary vein
   d. Vena Cava

2. How many squares in an ECG make up one minute of cardiac activity?

   a. 15
   b. 150
   c. 1500
   d. 300

3. Which part of the ECG records atrial repolarization?

   a. P wave
   b. QRS complex
   c. T wave
   d. U wave

UNIT IV : THE ACLS SURVEY

KEY 2020 GUIDELINE UPDATES

The AHA recommends that laypersons initiate CPR early for all presumed cases of cardiac arrest. The risk of harm to the patient is low, if the person is not actually in cardiac arrest.

Like BLS, ACLS follows a sequence of steps, referred to as the ACLS survey. These steps verify the actions taken during BLS, and refine them, if necessary. Earlier, this sequence was described as the A-B-C approach (Airway, Breathing, and Circulation). However, it is now recognized that maintaining blood circulation takes priority over oxygenation, as a patient generally has enough oxygen in the bloodstream to sustain the body for a few minutes. Therefore, the current approach is referred to as the C-A-B approach. The approach differs during BLS and ACLS, and these differences can be summarized in the table below:

Table 1. ACLS survey - initial and final steps

STEPS	INITIAL C-A-B-D STEPS (USUALLY UNDERTAKEN AS PART OF BLS)	ADVANCED CABD STEPS
C - Circulation	Chest compressions	Gain parenteral access to deliver ACLS medication
A - Airway	Basic airway management	Assess airway, perform advanced airway management
B - Breathing	Rescue breathing	Check for breath sounds Deliver 100% oxygen Capnography to assess CPR quality
D - Defibrillation; Differential diagnosis	Use of AED if available at the scene	Assess heart rhythm, use defibrillator as indicated Assess and treat reversible causes

CHAPTER 1

The Adult ACLS Algorithm

The adult ACLS algorithm is a series of steps which incorporate both initial and advanced CABD steps in a single, optimum pathway. The pathway described below is in accordance with the 2020 ACLS algorithm released by the AHA, and needs to be memorized by all ACLS providers.

ALGORITHM 2: ADULT ACLS ALGORITHM

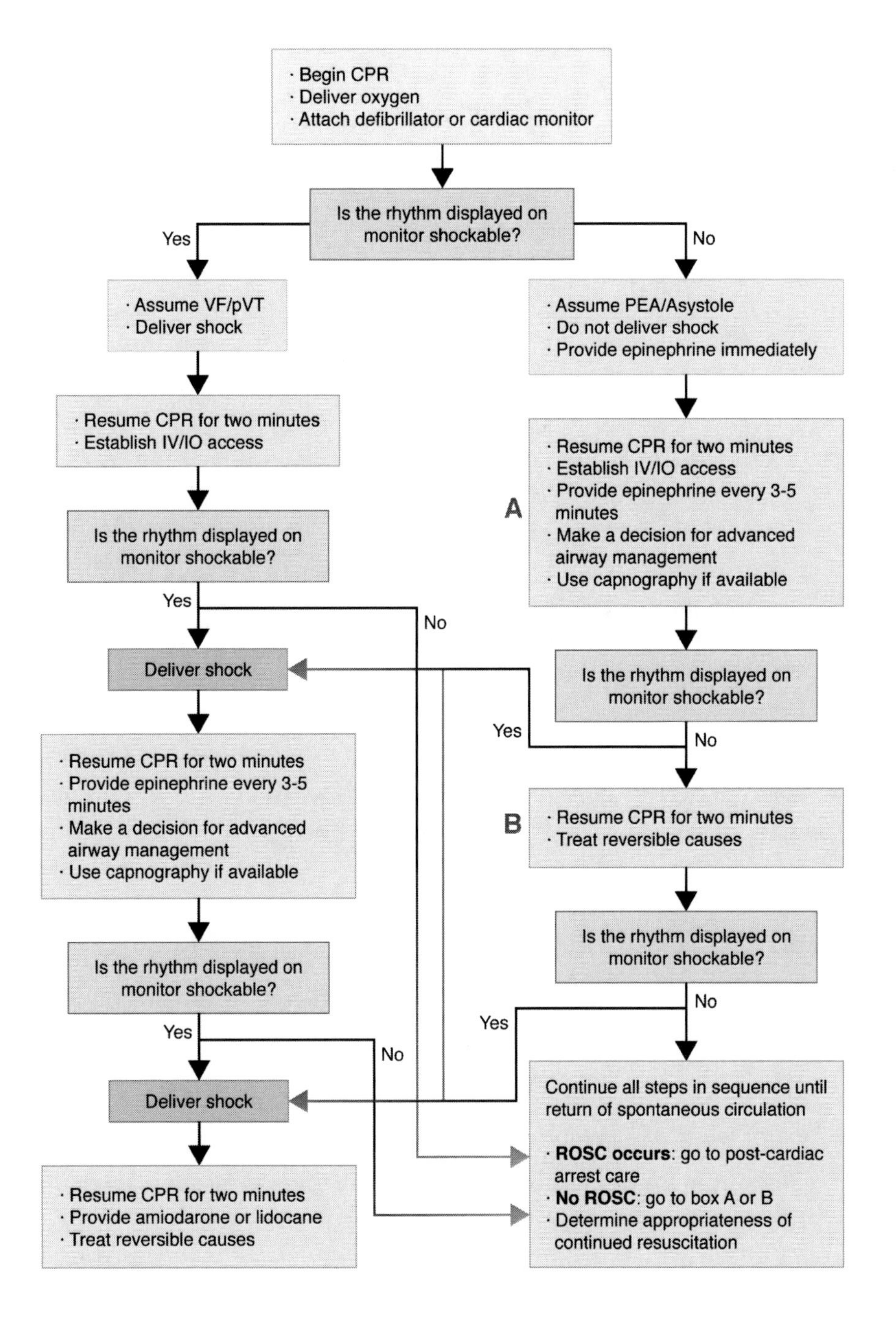

CHAPTER 2

ACLS Survey #1: Circulation

KEY 2020 GUIDELINE UPDATES

- o Physiological monitoring of CPR quality may be performed, using quantitative waveform capnography, or arterial blood pressure.
- o Intravenous access must be used for drug administration whenever possible. Intraosseous route is preferred only when IV access is unsuccessful or not feasible.

Maintaining circulation is the first and most important priority of ACLS. This is primarily achieved by chest compressions, and secondarily achieved by delivering vasopressor drugs and other medications into the circulatory system.

CHEST COMPRESSIONS:

This is part of the initial survey, and must be initiated by the first rescuer on the scene. Some rules to be kept in mind during chest compressions are:

- The depth of each compression must be at least 2 inches (5 cm).
- Complete chest recoil must occur after each compression.
- The compressions must be performed at a rapid rate of approximately 100 to 120 per minute.
- Prior to placing an advanced airway, the ratio of compressions to mouth breaths is 30:2.

- To avoid sub-optimal compressions due to fatigue, the rescuer performing compressions must switch over with the rescuer providing rescue breaths every 2 minutes.
- Unless absolutely necessary, chest compressions must not be interrupted, so as to avoid compromising perfusion.

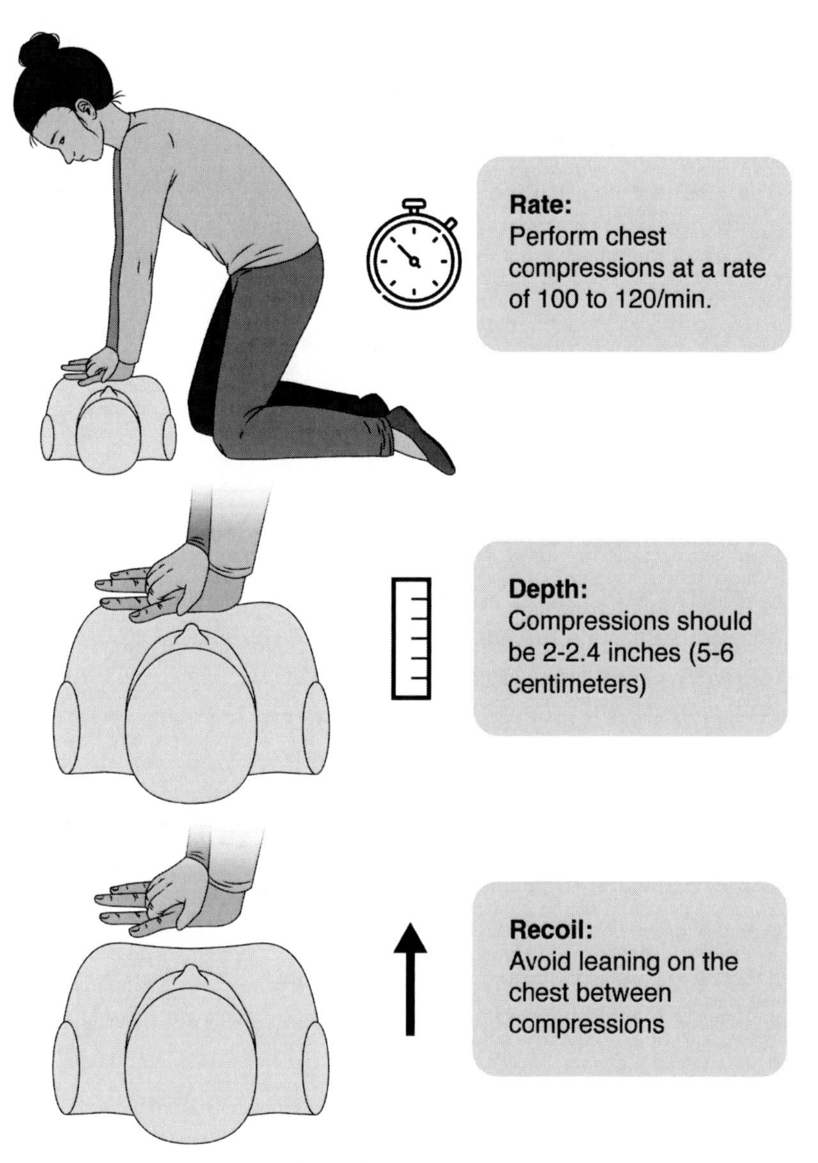

Figure 5. Rules for high-quality chest compressions.

Monitoring quality of CPR performed:

Real-time audiovisual feedback: Specific factors such as rate and depth of compressions must be consistently maintained in order to achieve high quality of compressions. While trained professionals may be consistently able to maintain such quality, inexperience or fatigue can cause an inadvertent decrease in compression quality. One way to maintain consistent quality of CPR is through real-time audiovisual feedback. Feedback devices are designed to measure CPR performance in real-time. Based on these measurements, audiovisual feedback is provided to the rescuer and guidance is offered to achieve the target depth and rate. The 2020 AHA guidelines suggest that it is reasonable to use these devices when available to optimize CPR quality.

Quantitative assessment: Quantitative methods also provide a means of assessing the quality of CPR provided. The 2020 AHA guidelines state that it is reasonable to use quantitative measures to assess CPR quality. This may be done by two methods:

- Quantitative waveform capnography: This is the preferred method to assess CPR quality and may be utilized if advanced airway management has been completed and an endotracheal tube has been placed. In capnography, a non-invasive sensor is used to continually measure values of end-tidal carbondioxide (ETCO2). ETCO2 refers to the maximal concentration of CO2 present at the end of an exhaled breath. Normal values in adults range from 35 – 45mmHg, and its values drop to zero when the heart stops beating. During CPR, the rescuer must attempt to maintain ETCO2 levels between 10 – 20mmHg.Values below 10mmHg indicate that the quality of chest compression needs to be improved.
- Arterial blood pressure: This may be utilized only if an arterial line is already in place. It may not be feasible to place an arterial line for monitoring alone, as this may cause unnecessary interruptions in CPR. If continuous arterial blood pressure monitoring is available, the rescuer should attempt to maintain the relaxation pressure values above 20mmHg.

SPECIALIZED CPR TECHNIQUES

Mechanical CPR:

- These are essentially automated devices that are capable of delivering high-quality chest compressions.
- Manual compressions are subject to decrease in quality due to fatigue and human error. It was assumed that these could be reduced with mechanical devices. However, studies have not proven superiority on these devices over manual CPR.
- The AHA does not recommend the routine use of mechanical CPR devices. However, these devices may be considered in settings where delivery of manual compressions is not feasible, or could be dangerous to the provider, for instance, in highly infectious patients, or if personnel are limited.

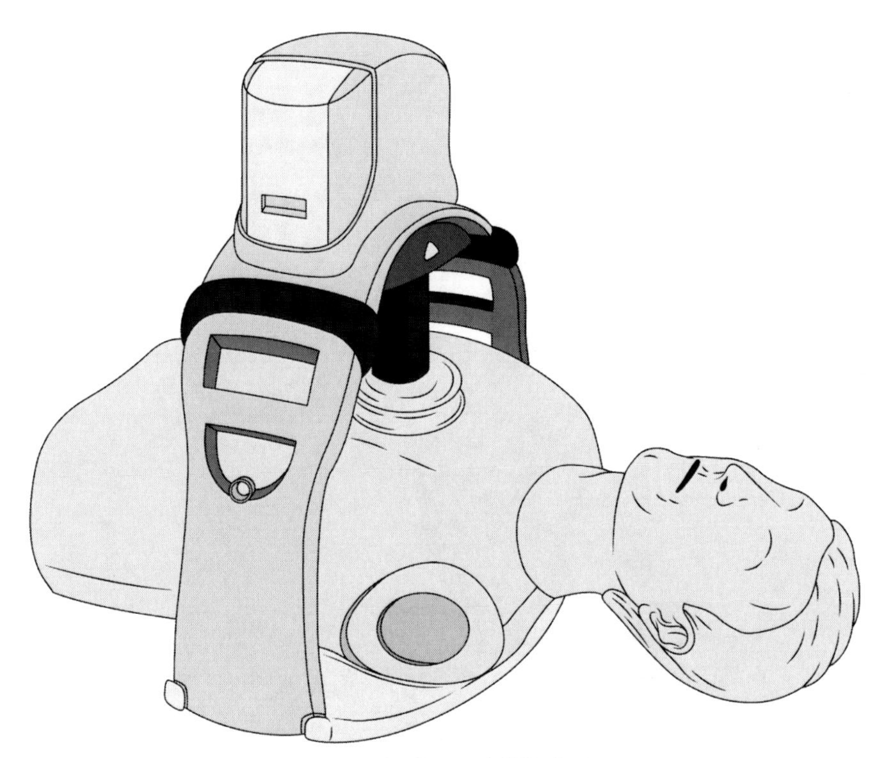

Figure 6. Mechanical CPR device

Active compression-decompression CPR with impedance threshold device:

- In the active compression-decompression technique, a handheld suction device is applied to the midsternum and held during chest compressions. This can potentially increase the negative intrathoracic pressure during each chest recoil, which in turn can improve venous return and cardiac output.
- An impedance threshold device consists of a pressure sensitive valve that is attached to the airway adjunct used – the face mask, or ET tube. During the decompression phase, air entry into the lungs is limited. This further increases the negative intrathoracic pressure during chest recoil.
- If rescuers are adequately trained in the use of both devices, the use of this technique may be considered. However, the impedance threshold device must not be combined with conventional CPR.

Figure 7. Active compression decompression CPR

Interposed abdominal compression CPR:

- This is a technique which can be carried out if three rescuers are available.
- This consists of conventional chest compressions, along with abdominal compressions. Separate rescuers perform the chest and abdominal compressions.
- The abdominal compression is performed by placing interlocked hands in the midline of the abdomen, between the xiphoid process and the umbilicus. Each compression is carried out during the recoil phase of the chest compression. These compressions increase venous return and coronary perfusion pressure.
- The AHA suggests that this technique be used if there are adequate personnel available who are trained in performing this technique.

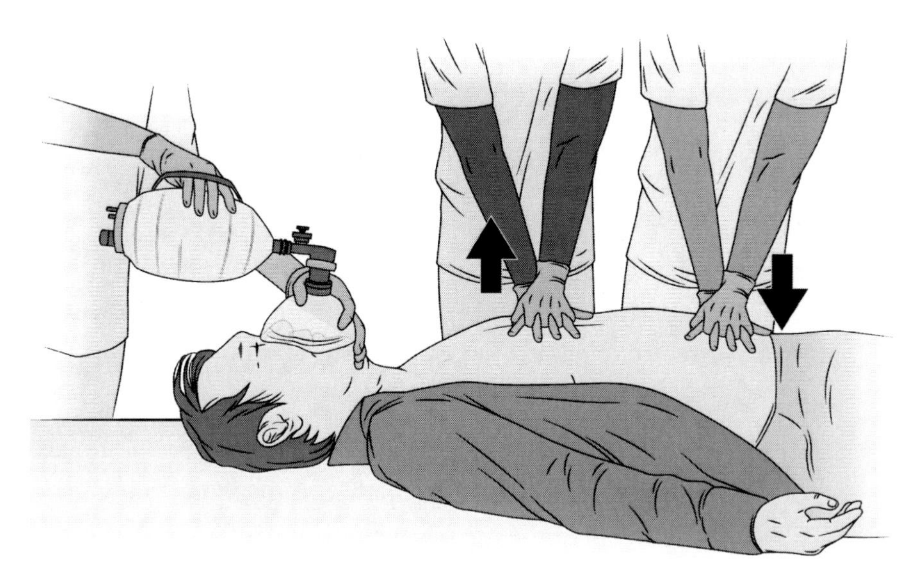

Figure 8. Interposed abdominal compression CPR

Extracorporeal CPR:

- This is a highly specialized technique which can only be performed if a skilled cardiovascular surgery team is available.
- The patient is placed on mechanical bypass. A large vein and artery are cannulated and the circulatory volume is subjected to extracorporeal circulation and membrane oxygenation (ECMO).
- The AHA does not usually recommend the use of extracorporeal CPR. It must only be considered for a selected group of patients where it is highly likely that the cause of arrest can be reversed during the limited period where bypass can be provided.

CIRCULATORY SUPPORT

ACLS requires the use of emergency pharmacotherapy. As soon as it is reasonable, a third rescuer (who is not providing either chest compressions or rescue breaths) must attempt to obtain circulatory access. This will allow the prompt delivery of life saving drugs.

ROUTES OF DRUG ACCESS:

Intravenous route:

- The intravenous route is the most preferred route of drug administration. The 2020 guidelines emphasize that the rescuers must first attempt to gain IV access for drug administration.
- Technique for IV access:
    - o Place the limb in a dependent position.
    - o To visualize the veins better, apply a tourniquet four to six inches proximal to the site of access. This helps dilate the vein. The tourniquet must not remain on longer than three minutes.
    - o Clean the access site with an antiseptic swab and maintain sterile technique throughout.
    - o Remove the cover from the IV needle and, using your dominant hand, hold with its bevel facing upwards. The needle should make a 45° angle with the skin.

  - Using your non-dominant hand, stretch the skin distal to the access site taut.
  - Pierce the skin and outer vein wall in a single motion. You will immediately see the 'flash' of blood in the chamber behind the hub. This indicates that the vein has been accessed.
  - Do not advance the needle further as this could result in a backwall puncture. Leaving the cannula in place, withdraw the needle alone from within the cannula. The cannula can then be advanced into the vein.
  - Secure the IV cannula in place with elastic adhesive plaster.
- Key points to remember when emergency drugs are given intravenously:
  - When drugs are given intravenously, the entire drug must be delivered as a bolus, and flush with 20ml of saline or any other IV fluid. To speed up the entry of the drug into circulation, the extremity at which the drug was given may be raised for 10 to 20 seconds.

Intraosseous route:

- According to the 2020 guidelines, intraosseous access may be attempted only when intravenous access is unsuccessful or not feasible. This is in contrast to earlier guidelines, which stated that IO access may be attempted if IV access was not readily available. If cardiac arrest is due to shock, however, it may be impossible to obtain veins for IV access due to peripheral vein collapse. The IO route offers a non-collapsible alternative in these cases.
- Technique for IO access:
  - The most convenient site for access is the anterior tibia.
  - Prepare the skin over the access site and maintain sterile technique throughout.
  - Take the intraosseous needle and hold it almost perpendicular to the skin and bone.
  - Insert it directly to pierce the skin and hit the bone.

- o Use a screwing motion once the bone is reached. This will facilitate bone entry. Once the bone marrow is entered, a sudden 'give' is encountered. Correct placement may be confirmed by aspirating bone marrow.
- o Remove the needle trocar and leave the cannula in place. Secure the cannula and attach the infusion set.

Other routes of access:

- Central venous access is another feasible technique in the hospital setting, provided that the rescue team has the skills and resources to perform the same. If a central line is already in place, however, it may be the preferred route for drug administration.
- The intracardiac route and endotracheal route were advocated historically; however, both routes are strongly discouraged today.
- The intracardiac route requires a highly specialized skill set and can have increased morbidity.
- The endotracheal route, while simple and convenient, results in very low blood concentrations and has unpredictable pharmacological effects.

DRUGS USED IN THE RESUSCITATION ALGORITHM:

Epinephrine:

- Epinephrine causes arteriolar constriction by stimulation of α-adrenergic receptors. This increases the pressure in the proximal aorta and shunts blood into the coronary arteries. This increases the chances of return of spontaneous circulation.
- Recommendations for administration of epinephrine:
  - o The 2020 AHA guidelines emphasize the importance of early administration of epinephrine. If a non-shockable rhythm is present, epinephrine must be administered as soon as possible. If a shockable rhythm is present, epinephrine must be administered after the first shock has been delivered.

  - o The dosage to be given is 1mg, in a dilution of 1:10,000 when given intravenously. This dose may be repeated every 3 to 5 minutes.
  - o The AHA does not recommend the use of high-dose epinephrine in cardiac arrest.
  - o Vasopressin has been considered previously as an alternative to epinephrine. The AHA does not recommend this, as there is no benefit to either substitution or addition of vasopressin to epinephrine.

Amiodarone:

- This is given in cardiac arrest associated with ventricular fibrillation or ventricular tachycardia. It has the effect of slowing down heart rhythm.
- Initially, a 300mg bolus dose is given intravenously. For subsequent doses, 150mg is given.

Lidocaine:

- This is another anti-arrythmic drug that can stabilize the heart rhythm. It may be used as an alternative to amiodarone in VF/VT.
- Initially, a loading dose of 1 to 1.5mg/kg may be given. The second dose is usually halved, and o.5 to 0.75 mg/kg may be given.
- Depending on rhythm changes and other cardiac parameters, several other drugs may be used.

Other drugs:

Various other drugs have been considered during CPR. These include steroids, calcium, magnesium, and sodium bicarbonate. However, after reviewing the available evidence, the AHA suggests that there is no benefit to the use of any of these drugs during CPR.

QUESTIONS

1. What is the level of ETCO2 that must be maintained during CPR?
   a. 5-10 mmHg
   b. 10-20 mmHg
   c. 20-30 mmHg
   d. 35-45 mmHg

2. What is the preferred route of drug administration?
   a. Intravenous
   b. Intraosseous
   c. Endotracheal
   d. Intracardiac

3. What is the dose of adrenaline to be given in cardiac arrest?
   a. 1 mg of 1 in 1000 dilution
   b. 1 mg of 1 in 10,000 dilution
   c. 0.5 mg of 1 in 1000 dilution
   d. 0.5 mg of 1 in 10000 dilution

4. Which drug is not recommended during cardiac arrest?
   a. Amiodarone
   b. Epinephrine
   c. Sodium bicarbonate
   d. Lidocaine

CHAPTER 3

ACLS Survey #2 & #3: Airway, Breathing, And Ventilation

The next step in the ACLS survey is ensuring that the patient has a clear, open airway. A patent airway is essential to ensure that ventilation and oxygenation can follow.

BASIC AIRWAY MANAGEMENT:

In the initial survey, basic airway management is done. This involves:

Head-tilt, chin-lift maneuver:

- Place one of your hands on the patient's forehead, and place the other hand beneath the chin, just under the bony part of the jaw.
- With one hand, tilt the patient's head backwards. Use the other hand to lift the lower jaw and draw the chin forward.
- Do not press too hard on the chin soft tissues as this might reflexively block the airway.
- Ensure that the patient's mouth remains partially open so that rescue breaths can be effectively delivered.
- Jaw-thrust maneuver is performed if the neck is immobilized or neck injury is suspected. Position yourself behind the patient. Rest your elbows on the firm surface on either side of the patient's head.

- Position your fingers under the patient's lower jaw, just behind the angle of the jaw. Lift the jaw manually with both hands, so that the jaw is thrust forward.

Suctioning:

- The airway may be obstructed by secretions such as saliva, blood, and vomitus. These can be evacuated using suction.
- A soft, flexible catheter must be used for suctioning. The catheter should be inserted to a comfortable depth within the oropharynx, and suctioning should be carried out while withdrawing the catheter.
- During the suctioning process, the patient cannot be ventilated, and oxygen cannot be administered. Therefore, this should only be carried out for 10 seconds at a time. Immediately after suctioning, ventilation must begin and the patient must be given 100% oxygen.
- Ideally, the patient must be monitored during suctioning. If the patient becomes cyanotic, or the saturation drops, suctioning must be interrupted and the patient must be ventilated immediately.

Placement of airway:

These are short tubes that are inserted through the oral or nasal cavity, and terminated at the pharynx. They help to keep the airway open and patent. They are of two types:

Oropharyngeal airway:

- This is a stiff, J-shaped plastic device which fits over the tongue into the pharynx. It can prevent tongue fall back and also push the soft palate away from the pharyngeal inlet.
- Indication: The oropharyngeal airway is only used when the patient is unresponsive. It may stimulate vomiting if the individual is conscious and has a gag reflex, which may lead to aspiration or laryngeal spasm.
- Technique of insertion:
    - o Clear secretions from the oral cavity and pharynx by suctioning.

- Select the appropriate size of airway by placing the device at the side of the patient's face, parallel to the sagittal plane. The device should ideally extend from the corner of the mouth to the earlobe.
- Insert the airway such that the concavity of the tube faces the roof of the mouth.
- After the device is completely inside, turn the tube so that the concavity now faces downwards. This will ensure that the tongue is not pushed back into the throat. Instead, it fits snugly into the concavity of the tube.

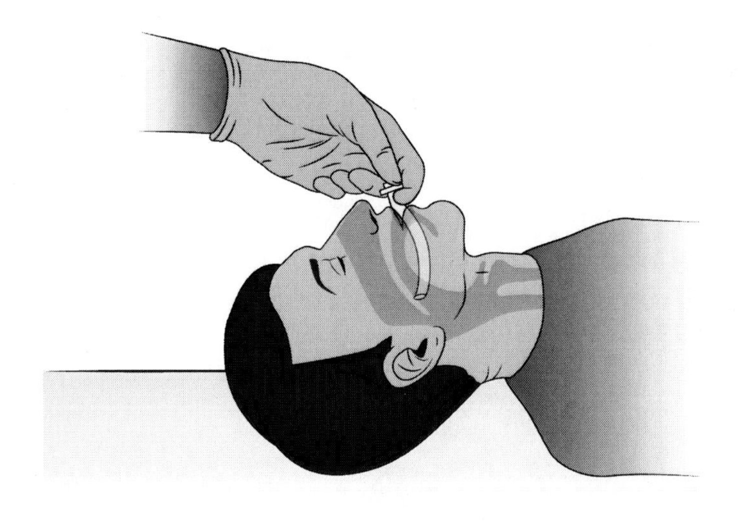

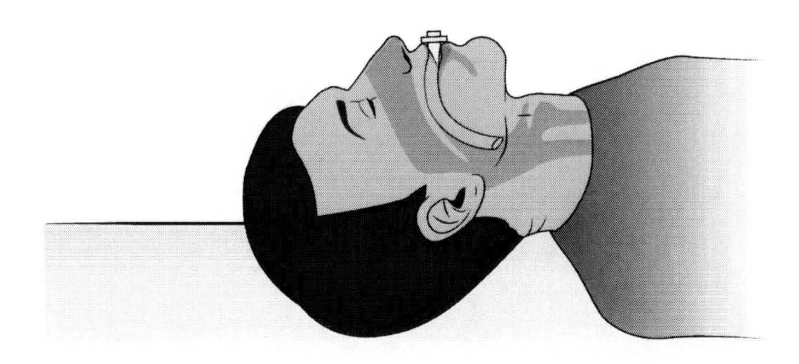

Figure 9. Technique of insertion of oropharyngeal airway

Nasopharyngeal airway:

- This is a flexible rubber or plastic tube which displaces the hypopharyngeal tissues and opens the airway.
- Indication: Unlike the oropharyngeal airway, this does not stimulate the gag reflex, and can hence be used in a conscious or semi-conscious patient.
- This airway is not preferred in patients with facial trauma as it may cause displacement of fractures.
- Technique for insertion:
  - o Select the appropriate size by holding the airway by the side of the face. The airway must extend from the tip of the nose to the earlobe.
  - o Lubricate the nostrils and the tube prior to insertion.
  - o Insert the tube in a single direction, so that its slight concavity faces downwards. This need not be turned after insertion.
  - o The airway must never be forced into the nostril. If force is encountered, the tube must be withdrawn and placement must be reattempted through the other nostril.

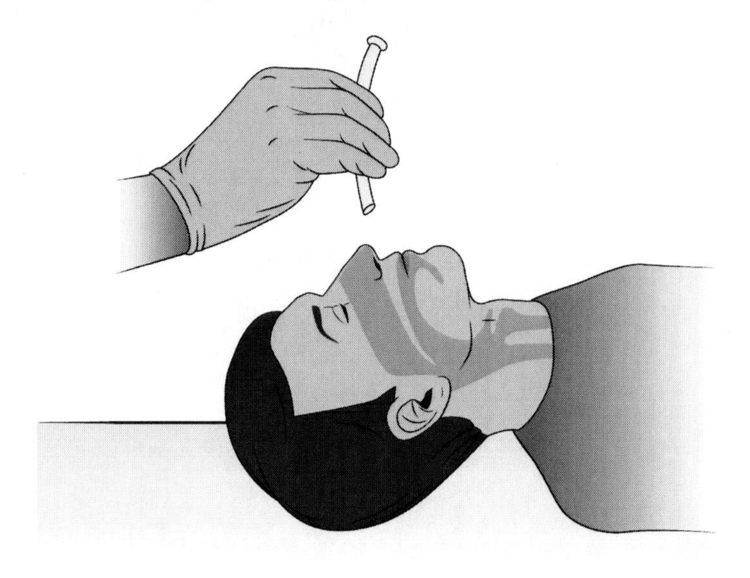

Figure 10a. Technique of insertion of nasopharyngeal airway.

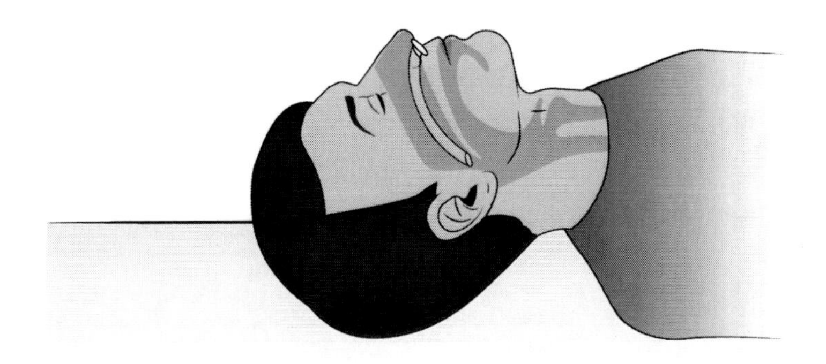

Figure 10b. Technique of insertion of nasopharyngeal airway.

VENTILATION DURING BASIC AIRWAY MANAGEMENT:

- During the initial survey, rescue breathing is performed, using either mouth-to-mouth resuscitation, mouth-to-mask ventilation, or bag-mask ventilation.
- During bag-mask ventilation, attempt to deliver a volume of 500ml to 600ml with each breath. Since the ambu-bag is about 1 to 2 liters, it should ideally be compressed to only one-fourth to half of its capacity.
- When ventilation is performed with a basic airway, provide 2 rescue breaths for every 30 compressions. Each breath must be delivered over one second.
- Checking for chest rise and fall is a good guide to ensure that ventilation is adequate. Over-ventilation must be avoided, as it can increase the intrathoracic pressure, and impede venous return to the heart.
- Provide 100% oxygen as soon as it becomes available. Oxygen saturation must be monitored through a pulse oximeter, and the saturation must be maintained at or above 94%.

ADVANCED AIRWAY MANAGEMENT

Advanced airway management must be attempted only if bag-mask ventilation is deemed to be inadequate. The need for an advanced airway must be balanced against the risk of interrupting CPR. On the other hand, advanced airway placement can help evaluate the quality of CPR using waveform capnography.

Endotracheal tube:

- An endotracheal (ET) tube is a rigid tube that goes from the oral cavity down into the trachea. It has an inflatable cuff at its lower end, which stabilizes the tube.
- The placement of an ET tube requires technical skill; however, this is the best option for advanced airway as it is the most secure and can ensure most effective ventilation. An ET tube allows for controlled ventilation and can prevent aspiration of gastric contents into the lungs.
- An ET tube must be placed under direct vision. To visualize the laryngeal inlet and vocal cords, a blade-like device called the laryngoscope is used.
- Steps in ET tube placement:
    - Position the patient supine, with the neck extended (sniffing position). Provide oxygen and ventilation until the moment the ET tube is ready to be inserted.
    - Choose the appropriate size. In general, adult men will require sizes between 7.5 and 8, while adult women will require sizes between 7 and 7.5. The smaller the stature of the individual, smaller will be the tube size.
    - Check the tube for leaks by inflating the cuff. Deflate the cuff prior to insertion, and lubricate the tube.
    - Open the patient's mouth using the thumb and index finger of the right hand. Use your left hand to pick up the laryngoscope.
    - Insert the laryngoscope blade at the right corner of the mouth, and rotate it so that the curvature of the blade fits on the

posterior part of the tongue. Use the blade to 'lift' the posterior tongue and faucial pillars out of the way, so that the epiglottis and laryngeal inlet can be visualized.

- o Use suction to clear secretions if needed. Under direct vision, pick up the ET tube with your right hand and pass it through the laryngeal inlet into the trachea. If the laryngeal inlet is not easily visible, you can ask for cricoid pressure. Applying pressure to the cricoid cartilage pushes the laryngeal inlet posteriorly and superiorly, allowing better vision.
- o Once the ET tube is in place, the cuff may be inflated. Confirm tracheal placement by ventilating with an ambu-bag, and auscultating for breath sounds. Correct positioning can also be confirmed by quantitative waveform capnography.

- The biggest drawback to ET tube placement is that it is a technique-sensitive skill and can only be carried out successfully by individuals who are well-trained and perform intubations frequently. Due to these limitations, other alternatives have emerged for advanced airway management.

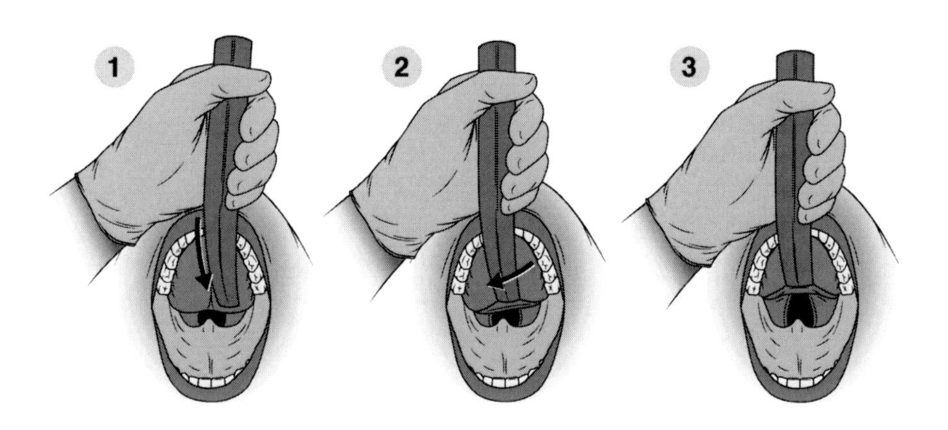

Figure 11. Insertion of laryngoscope to view epiglottis and laryngeal inlet

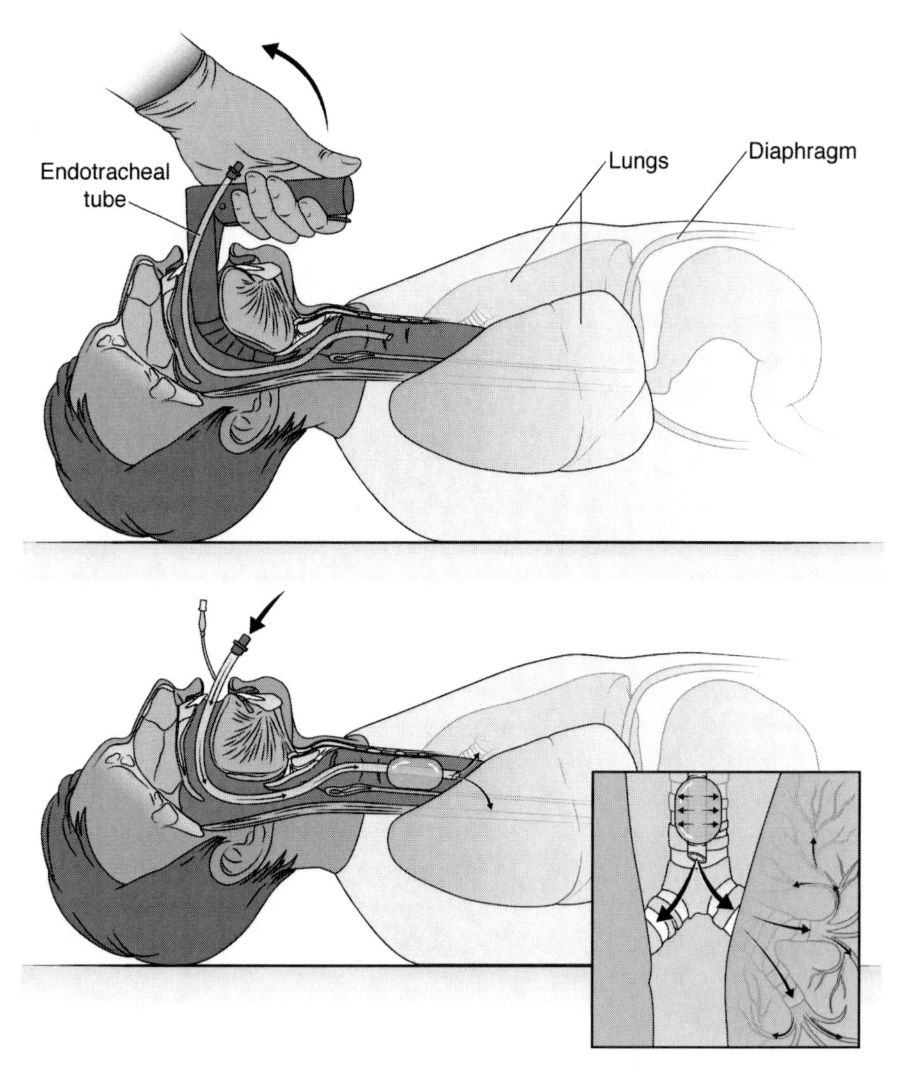

Figure 12. Technique of tube placement

Laryngeal mask airway (LMA)

- This is an alternative to the ET tube. It can provide comparative ventilation and is simpler to place.
- It is preferable when a laryngoscope is not available, or access to the airway is limited. For instance, when a neck injury is suspected and the neck cannot be extended.
- The LMA consists of a small mask-shaped aperture called the cuff, which is designed to fit snugly over the laryngeal inlet. The cuff connects to a semi-rigid airway tube. A second, more flexible tube connects to the cuff and is used to inflate it. The flexible tube as an inflation indicator and a pilot balloon to check extent of inflation.
- Steps for insertion of LMA:
    - o Position the patient supine, with the head slightly extended. Provide ventilation and oxygenation until the LMA is prepared.
    - o Choose the appropriate size of LMA. As a general guide, size 5 fits most adult men while size 4 fits women. Check the LMA for leaks by inflating the cuff.
    - o Deflate the cuff against a flat surface and lubricate the posterior part of the cuff alone. Lubricating the entire tube may occlude it and cause airway obstruction.
    - o Insert the cuffed end of the LMA through the oral cavity into the pharynx. The cuff aperture must face the tongue. Continue insertion until resistance is encountered.
    - o The LMA may be inserted blindly. Use of cricoid pressure is not advisable, as it may lead to improper positioning once the pressure is removed, decreasing the efficiency of ventilation.
    - o Inflate the cuff. This pushes it against the laryngeal opening and creates a snug seal against it, allowing air to be delivered directly into the trachea.
    - o Insert a bite block to prevent the possibility of patient biting down on the tube and causing airway obstruction.

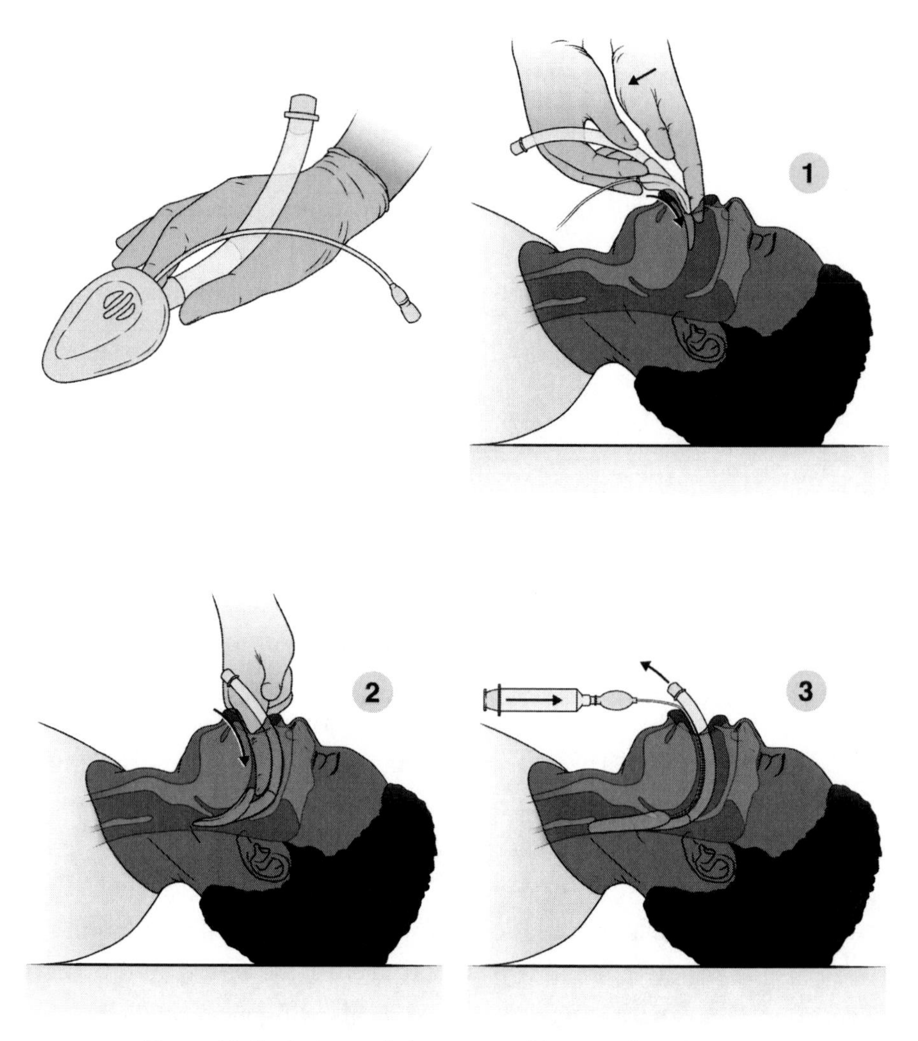

Figure 13. Technique of placement of laryngeal mask airway

Laryngeal tube:

- This is also an acceptable alternative to the ET tube for ventilation during cardiac arrest. It is a smaller, more compact tube which terminates at the supraglottic region. This is a simple tube which has two cuffs – an oropharygngeal cuff, which is present in the middle of the tube, and an esophageal cuff, which is located at the terminal end of the tube.
- Steps for insertion of the laryngeal tube:
    - o Position the patient, provide ventilation and oxygenation.
    - o As with other devices, select the appropriate size and check tube integrity.
    - o The tube must be guided along the hard palate, and from there into the posterior part of the oropharynx until resistance is encountered.
    - o The end of the laryngeal tube must be positioned just at the upper end of the laryngeal inlet.

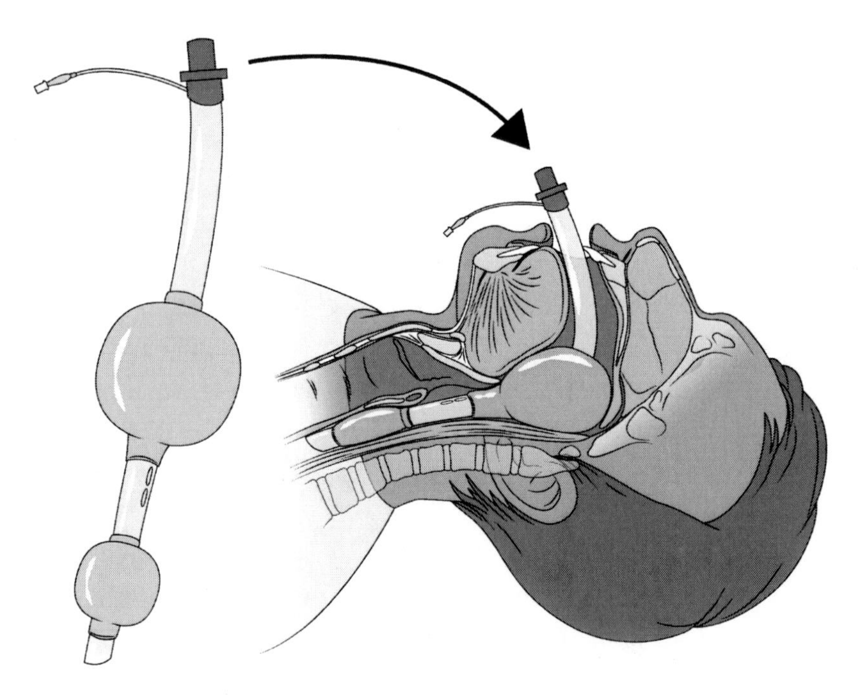

Figure 14. Laryngeal tube placement

Combitube:

- This is also known as the esophageal-tracheal tube. This is a double lumen tube, which has two inlets at the outer end – the pharyngeal inlet and esophageal inlet. The proximal, or the pharyngeal lumen terminates at the beginning of the laryngeal inlet. The distal lumen terminates in the upper part of the esophagus. The distal lumen has an inflatable cuff at the terminal end, which can protect against aspiration of gastric contents. The combitube also has a larger proximal cuff which is designed to occlude the hypopharynx.
- Steps for insertion of combitube:
    - Position the patient, provide ventilation and oxygenation.
    - Select the appropriate size and check tube integrity in both cuffs.
    - Position the tube such that the curvature of the tube matches the curvature of the pharynx. The proximal lumen should face the back of the throat, while the distal lumen faces the front of the throat and tongue. The bifurcated end is the outermost component.
    - Advance the tube till the markings on the tube are positioned between the front teeth. Inflate both the cuffs. Now, the location of the tube has to be confirmed. In most cases, this will rest just above the laryngeal inlet but rarely, it can lie within the esophagus. This may be confirmed by attaching the ambu-bag to one of the two inlets.
    - First attach the ambu-bag to the esophageal inlet and squeeze it. If you can auscultate breath sounds, it indicates that the tip of the tube is in the esophagus. Use the esophageal inlet for ventilation; air will be delivered to the trachea via openings in the side of the tube.
    - If no breath sounds are heard, transfer the ambu-bag to the pharyngeal inlet and squeeze. Breath sounds should be heard now, which indicates that the tube tip is at the opening of the

laryngeal inlet. Ventilate through the pharyngeal inlet; air will directly be delivered through the lumen tip.

- As with LMA, cricoid pressure must not be applied during insertion of the combitube.
- The combitube is not generally preferred over other options, as it has the potential to cause esophageal injury. It also comes in limited sizes and cannot be used for pediatric patients or patients with short stature.

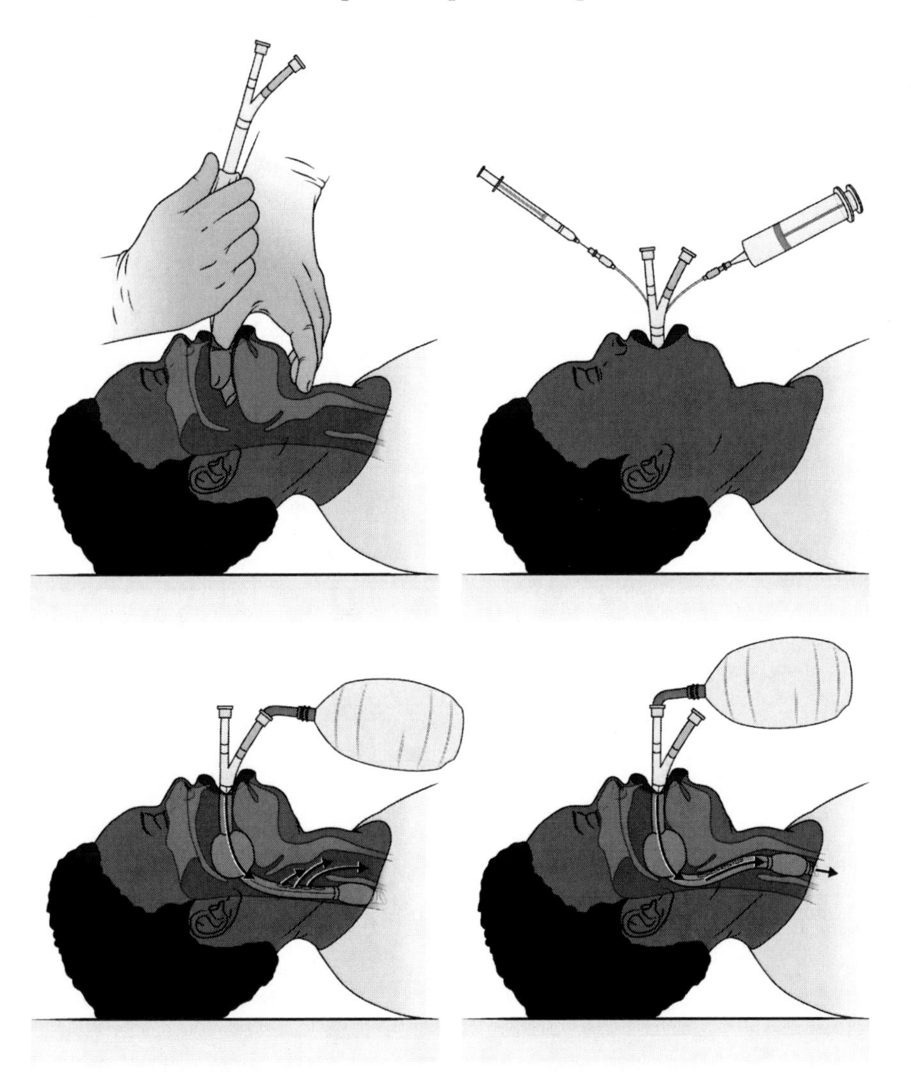

Figure 15. Steps in insertion of combitube

VENTILATION DURING ADVANCED AIRWAY MANAGEMENT

- After any type of advanced airway placement, use waveform capnography to confirm that the airway is in place, and to monitor CPR quality thereafter.
- Most of the rules followed during basic ventilation apply during ventilation with an advanced airway as well.
- When an advanced airway is in place, the 30:2 rule need not be followed any longer, as in all probability there are more rescuers. Provide continuous chest compressions, except during switching over and defibrillation, and deliver continuous, asynchronous ventilations once every six seconds.

QUESTIONS

1. Which of the following is not part of basic airway management?
   a. Suctioning
   b. Jaw thrust maneuver
   c. Laryngeal mask airway
   d. Nasopharyngeal airway

2. What is the volume of air that must be delivered with each rescue breath?
   a. 200 to 300 ml
   b. 500 to 600 ml
   c. 700 to 800 ml
   d. 1000 to 1200 ml

3. Which of the following airway techniques require direct visualization of the respiratory passage during insertion?
   a. Endotracheal intubation
   b. Laryngeal mask airway placement
   c. Laryngeal tube placement
   d. Combitube placement

CHAPTER 4

ACLS Survey #4: Defibrillation

While CPR can sustain life by artificially circulating blood in the body, it cannot restore the original rhythm of the heart. In certain scenarios, this may be achieved by defibrillation. Defibrillation delivers an electric shock to the heart, which stimulates the sinoatrial node into regaining its normal rhythm. Studies have shown that using defibrillators, when combined with CPR, can improve survival rate by as much as 75%.

TYPES OF DEFIBRILLATORS:

Based on their intended purpose, there are essentially five different types of defibrillators. It is important for life providers to be aware of the different kinds, so that the appropriate defibrillator can be selected for use in an emergency.

Automated External Defibrillator (AED):

These are portable defibrillators, which are designed for use by lay individuals. It is extremely user-friendly, and the rescuer merely turns the device on and follows a series of prompts that are issued. The AED can automatically detect the heart rhythm and analyze whether the rhythm is shockable or not. Accordingly, the user receives a prompt to deliver shock or proceed with CPR.

Implantable Cardioverter Defibrillator (ICD):

This defibrillator is designed to be implanted surgically into the patient's body. When they detect abnormal rhythms, they send out a shock that restores rhythm to normal. ICDs are used in patients who are at high risk of developing cardiac arrest.

Wearable Cardioverter Defibrillator (WCD):

This is similar to an ICD, except that instead of being implanted surgically in the body, this is a vest-like device which can be worn on the outside. WCDs are used for patients in whom the risk of cardiac arrest is high for a short period of time – such as after cardiac bypass surgery, or just following a myocardial infarction.

Manual external defibrillators:

These defibrillators are more efficient than all the other kinds of defibrillators and are the most preferred in cases of cardiac arrest, assuming the rescuer is trained to use it. These are usually used in conjunction with electrocardiograms. While the ECG records the heart rhythm, it is up to the rescuer to analyze the rhythm and deliver shock using the defibrillator if appropriate.

The manual defibrillator is more efficient than an AED largely because the rescuer can assess a rhythm and take action at a much faster rate than the AED can analyze the rhythm. However, there is always the risk that a rescuer can deliver an inappropriate shock. Therefore, it is very important for ACLS rescuers to be well-trained in assessing ECG rhythms. Manual defibrillators may be external and internal. External defibrillators are used more often when cardiac arrest occurs outside or within the hospital settings. Internal defibrillators are used during open heart surgery, and the paddles can directly be used on the heart.

Based on the pattern of current flow, there are two types of manual defibrillators:

- **Monophasic defibrillator:** These are the conventional defibrillators. The current flows in a single direction, from an electrode on one side of the patient's chest to the other. For monophasic defibrillators, the current needs to be high enough to interrupt the abnormal rhythm, but at the same time, it is important to avoid extremely high current, which could potentially cause morphological damage to the heart. The AHA recommends that a shock of 360J be delivered during defibrillation.
- **Biphasic defibrillator:** These defibrillators were developed more recently, based on the design of the implantable defibrillators. The current flows in two directions, from each electrode to the other. This helps achieve the same effect but at lower energy levels. For biphasic defibrillators, the AHA suggests following manufacturer instructions. The initial dose is usually 120 to 200J. Subsequent doses must either be equivalent to this or higher. If the manufacturer instructions are unknown, the maximum available dose is usually used. The AHA prefers the use of biphasic defibrillators over monophasic when available, as they have greater efficiency in terminating arrhythmias.

KEY POINTS TO REMEMBER WHILE USING A DEFIBRILLATOR:

Timing of defibrillation:

- It is essential that defibrillation be immediately preceded and succeeded by CPR. If defibrillation is done before CPR even begins, the heart energy reserves may be depleted and the efficacy of defibrillation may be compromised. CPR will help replenish these reserves prior to defibrillation.
- However, if the onset of VF/VT is witnessed by the provider, with the defibrillator pads already applied, then defibrillation may be

provided first. In such cases, the heart has not been in arrest for long and should have adequate energy reserves.

- Research shows that the survival rate significantly increases to 50% if defibrillation is provided within 5 minutes from the onset of sudden cardiac arrest. After this time frame, survival rate decreases to 7 to 10% for each minute that the patient stays in cardiac arrest.
- After defibrillation, it is preferable to resume CPR immediately rather than performing a post-shock rhythm analysis. Even if defibrillation was successful, there might be a short period of asystole or pulseless electrical activity. CPR can again help restore energy and maintain perfusion in these scenarios. CPR must only be paused if there is physiological evidence of ROSC by capnography or arterial blood pressure.

Number of shocks and magnitude:

- In their 2020 guidelines, the AHA recommends a single shock strategy rather than a series of 'stacked' shocks with progressively higher energy levels. This is because when biphasic defibrillators are used, there is a high rate of rhythm reversal in the first attempt. Stacked shocks necessitate greater interruptions in CPR, which may compromise survival.
- There is no optimal energy setting and the AHA recommends following manufacturer instructions for the same, or using the maximal dose if this information is not available.
- The 2020 guidelines do not advocate the use of double sequential defibrillation, as there is currently little evidence to support its use. Double sequential defibrillation is the process of using two defibrillators simultaneously to deliver maximal energy at the same time.

Defibrillation pads:

- The defibrillation pads may be placed in any one of the following positions: anterolateral, anteroposterior, anterior- left infrascapular, or anterior- right infrascapular. The AHA recommends that the pads or paddles used should be at least 8-12cm in diameter, to reduce transthoracic impedance.

- Either adhesive pads or paddles may be used. Adhesive pads may be preferable because they allow better skin contact, which might improve the efficacy of defibrillation.

Special considerations:

- Defibrillation in a wet patient: If the patient has been lying in snow or water, the chest region may be wet. In this case, time must be taken to quickly wipe the chest dry prior to proceeding with defibrillation. Defibrillating in a wet patient may lead to electrical injury.
- Chest hair: Adhesive pads may not stick to the skin if chest hair is present. In these cases, it may be preferable to use paddles if present, or quickly shave the chest hair prior to applying adhesive pads.
- Implantable pacemakers or defibrillators: These are palpable as hard masses beneath the skin. They can block the energy of the defibrillator shock. Therefore, avoid placing the defibrillator pads directly over these devices. Keep at least a distance of 1 inch (2.5 cm).
- Transdermal patches: Several patients use transdermal patches for medications such as nitroglycerin, hormones, and nicotine. These patches, if present, may block delivery of electric current to the heart, and can even cause skin burns. Remove any visible transdermal patches and wipe the area clean before defibrillating.

PSEUDOELECTRIC ALTERNATIVES TO DEFIBRILLATION

In the absence of defibrillation, several pseudoelectric therapies have been considered as alternatives. The 2020 AHA guidelines have reviewed the utility of each of these measures. They are summarized in the table below.

PSEUDOELECTRIC ALTERNATIVE	DESCRIPTION	RECOMMENDATION
Precordial thump	A single, sharp impact or 'punch' to the mid-sternum. The fist must be tightly clenched and impact delivered using the ulnar side. This may deliver a low energy shock to the heart.	May be considered when the rescuer witnesses the onset of an unstable tachyarrythmia, and defibrillator is not immediately available. Should not delay CPR or defibrillation Not to be used in established cardiac arrest
Transcutaneous pacing	Temporary method of pacing the heart. This is achieved by delivering electric current from a pacemaker via ECG leads	Not recommended during cardiac arrest as it may interfere with delivery of CPR.
Percussion pacing	Delivery of a continuous low level impact to the sternum using a closed fist. This attempts to simulate an electric impulse that can cause myocardial depolarization.	Temporization measure if there is a witnessed in-hospital arrest in a patient who is being monitored, and rhythm shows bradyasystole. Must not delay definitive therapy
Cough CPR	Requires a conscious, cooperative patient; this consists of repeated deep breaths followed by cough. This aims at increasing aortic and intracardiac pressure, which can provide some degree of hemodynamic support.	When there is witnessed onset of bradyarrythmia or tachyarrythmia, prior to loss of consciousness Must not delay definitive treatment

QUESTIONS

1. Which is the most preferred defibrillator during the ACLS protocol?
   a. Automated external defibrillator
   b. Manual monophasic defibrillator
   c. Manual biphasic defibrillator
   d. Implantable cardioverter defibrillator

2. What is the accepted energy setting for a monophasic manual defibrillator?
   a. 120J
   b. 200J
   c. 260J
   d. 360J

3. What is the acceptable size for a defibrillator pad in an adult patient?
   a. 5 to 6 cm
   b. 7 to 9 cm
   c. 8 to 12 cm
   d. 12 to 15 cm

4. Which of the following pseudoelectric techniques can only be performed in a conscious patient?
   a. Precordial thump
   b. Percussion pacing
   c. Transcutaneous pacing
   d. Cough CPR

CHAPTER 5

Recognizing Different Cardiac Arrest Rhythms

Prior to defibrillation, it is important to assess the cardiac rhythm on the ECG monitor. The type of cardiac rhythm will dictate the next step, either to proceed with defibrillation or continue with CPR.

SHOCKABLE RHYTHMS:

Two specific conditions have shockable rhythms – ventricular fibrillation and ventricular tachycardia. These are described in detail below:

Ventricular fibrillation

In ventricular fibrillation, cardiac impulses are rapid and erratic. This leads to rapid quivering of the ventricular walls, which are unable to contract enough to pump blood. It is common following a heart attack, but can also occur secondary to diseases of the heart muscle or valves, drug toxicity, or sepsis.

On the ECG, the following characteristics are seen:

- Rhythm: Rhythm is not regular and extremely disorganized
- Rate: Rate appears to be rapid but is unmeasurable.
- Waves: The P wave is absent. QRS complex and T waves cannot be distinguished from each other and are highly variable. Duration of PR interval, QRS complex, and QT intervals are unmeasurable.

The ECG waves may appear to be coarse or fine. Coarse VF is indicative of more electrical activity. As VF progresses and acidosis and hypoxia develop, the waves become finer and eventually may lead to asystole.

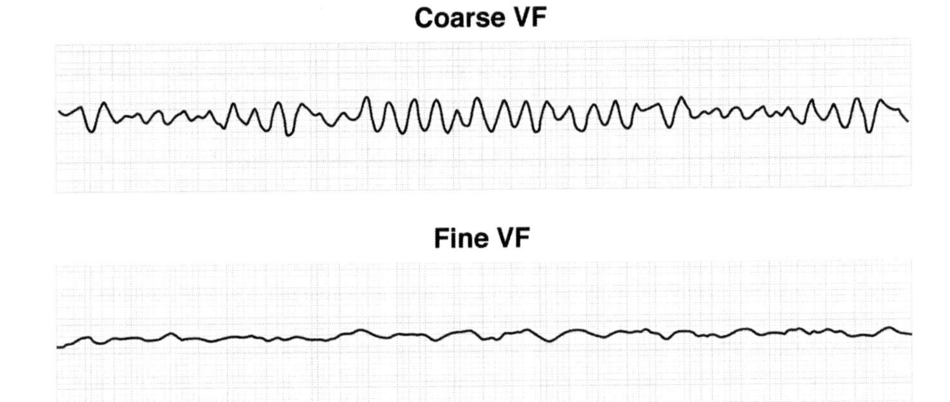

Figure 16. ECG pattern in Ventricular fibrillation.

Ventricular tachycardia:

VT may occur following a heart attack, or diseases of the heart valves or muscles. It can also occur in cardiac failure. In VT, the rapid heartbeat prevents the heart from emptying completely before it is filled again. This impedes cardiac output.

- Rhythm: Ventricular rhythm is usually regular, but may sometimes be irregular. Atrial rhythm is not measurable because P waves are absent.
- Rate: The ventricular rate may range from 150 to 250 beats per minute. Again atrial rate cannot be measured as P waves are absent.
- Waves: P waves are usually absent. In case they are present, they may be dissociated from the QRS complex or may be retrograde. QRS complexes are wide and may have a bizzare shape. The duration and amplitude is increased. QRS complex may be merged with the T wave, which occurs in the opposite direction.

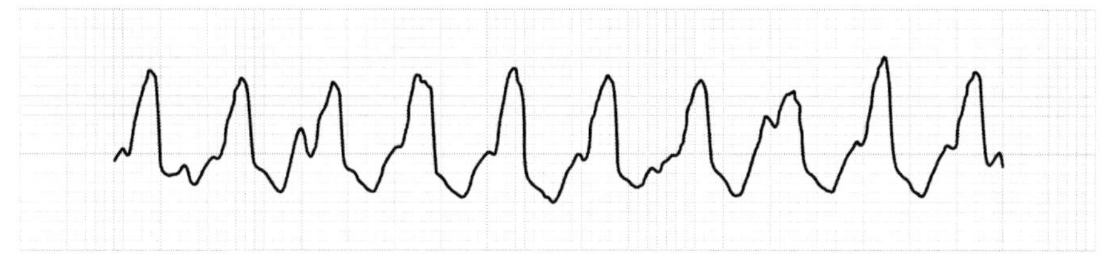

Figure 17. ECG pattern for ventricular tachycardia

NON-SHOCKABLE RHYTHMS:

In two specific rhythms of cardiac arrest, defibrillation must not be performed. These two rhythms include pulseless electrical activity and asystole.

Pulseless Electrical Activity (PEA)

In this condition, a pulse is not palpable, although the ECG shows some organized electrical activity. This is also known as electromechanical dissociation. The most common causes of PEA are hypovolemia and hypoxia. If PEA is not addressed immediately, it eventually leads to asystole in a few minutes. The electrical activity seen in PEA is highly variable and usually reflects the underlying rhythm.

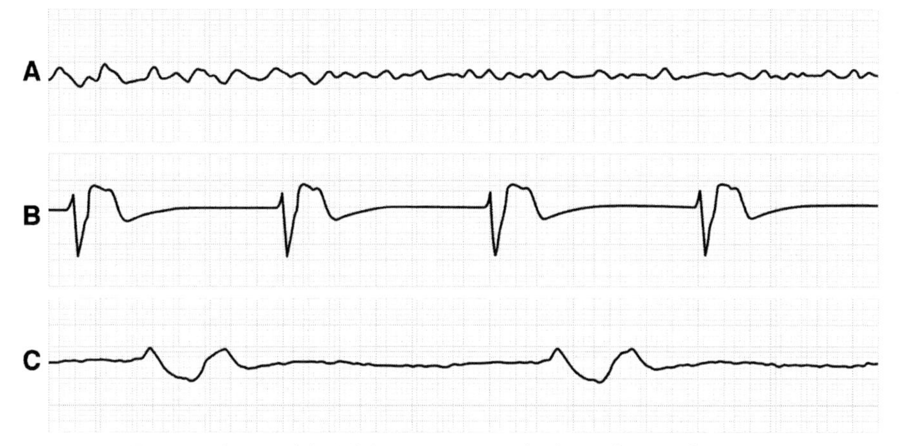

Figure 18. Variable ECG pattens in pulseless electrical activity

Asystole

Asystole refers to a complete flatline on the ECG monitor. It reflects a complete absence of ventricular activity – since there is absolutely no ventricular contraction, there is no cardiac output. No rhythm or rate is discernible. P waves, QRS complexes, and T waves are absent. The PR and QT intervals are therefore not measurable.

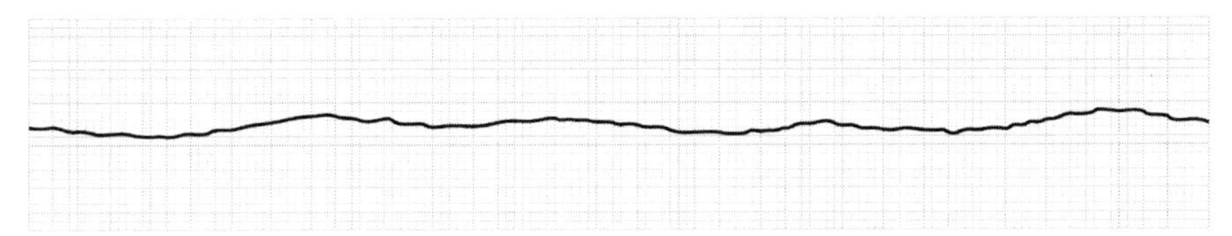

Figure 19. ECG pattern in asystole

QUESTIONS

1. What is the heart rate seen in ventricular tachyarrythmia?
   a. 50 to 100 beats per minute
   b. 100 to 150 beats per minute
   c. 150 to 250 beats per minute
   d. 300 to 400 beats per minute

2. What is the commonest cause of pulseless electrical activity?
   a. Hypokalemia
   b. Hypovolemia
   c. Cardiac tamponade
   d. Tension pneumothorax

3. In which of the following conditions is cardiac contraction completely absent?
   a. Ventricular fibrillation
   b. Ventricular tachycardia
   c. Pulseless electrical activity
   d. Asystole

CHAPTER 6

Other Considerations in The ACLS Algorithm

DIFFERENTIAL DIAGNOSIS:

The second 'D' in the advanced survey refers to differential diagnosis. Depending on the patient's medical history and the circumstances in which arrest occurred, the most likely diagnosis must be considered and addressed. Specific case scenarios that are likely to lead to cardiac arrest are discussed in Unit VI.

5Hs	5Ts
• Hypovolemia	• Tension pneumothorax
• Hypoxia	• Tamponade, cardiac
• Hydrogen ion acidosis	• Thrombosis, pulmonary
• Hypothermia	• Thrombosis, cardiac
• Hypo/hyperkalemia	• Toxins

WHEN MUST CPR BE TERMINATED?

The decision to stop CPR is made during one of the following two scenarios:

A. Return of spontaneous circulation (ROSC):

ROSC implies that the patient's heart starts beating effectively on its own again, and CPR is no longer necessary to sustain life. The following parameters are indicative that ROSC has occurred:

- Visible pulse and blood pressure on the monitor
- Visible arterial pressure waves on the intra-arterial monitor
- ETCO2 values abruptly increase, usually to values above 40mmHg.

B. Stopping CPR when ROSC has not been attained:

The duration of CPR in the absence of ROSC has been an ongoing debate.

Terminating resuscitation in the field:

The AHA guidelines recommend that in the field, the BLS or ALS termination of resuscitation rules must be followed prior to shifting the patient to an ambulance for transport.

BLS termination of resuscitation (TOR) rules: TOR must be considered if all the following criteria are met:

- The EMS provider did not witness the cardiac arrest
- There is no ROSC
- No shock has been delivered

ALS TOR rules: TOR must be considered if all the following criteria are met:

- EMS provider did not witness the arrest
- The patient did not receive bystander CPR
- No ROSC after complete ACLS care was provided

- No shock was delivered.

Terminating in-hospital resuscitation:

- For in-hospital resuscitation, in most scenarios, the patient is intubated. Therefore, ETCO2 may be used as a prognostic indicator for considering TOR. The AHA guidelines suggest that, in an intubated patient, if the ETCO2 has been less than 10mmHg, after resuscitating for more than 20 minutes, this may be considered as an indicator of TOR along with other multimodal approaches.
- Point-of-care ultrasound may also be used to evaluate blood flow and perfusion following cardiac arrest.

QUESTIONS

1. Which of the following is not a likely cause of cardiac arrest?

    a. Hypothermia
    b. Hyperthermia
    c. Hypokalemia
    d. Hyperkalemia

2. Which value of ETCO2 indicates a return of spontaneous circulation?

    a. 30 mmHg
    b. 40 mmHg
    c. 50 mmHg
    d. 60 mmHg

3. For terminating in-hospital resuscitation, the ETCO2 level must have been less than 10 mmHg for what duration of time?

    a. 10 minutes
    b. 20 minutes
    c. 30 minutes
    d. 40 minutes

UNIT V : POST-CARDIAC ARREST CARE

KEY 2020 GUIDELINE UPDATES

- o There is a need for multimodal rehabilitation assessment and treatment. This should include treatment for physical, cardiopulmonary, neuronal, and cognitive impairments.
- o Survivors and caregivers should receive a multidisciplinary discharge plan, and structured assessment for anxiety, depression, fatigue, and post-traumatic stress.
- o Rescuers, EMS providers, and hospital healthcare workers must receive a debriefing and referral for follow up

Post cardiac-arrest care begins the moment return of spontaneous circulation occurs. While the ACLS algorithm is responsible for saving an individual's life, proper post-cardiac arrest care can ensure that the individual attains a decent quality of life following cardiac arrest. In 2020, the AHA developed several recommendations and put forth an algorithm for post-cardiac arrest care. They recommend that post-cardiac arrest care must follow a comprehensive, multidisciplinary, structured approach.

The goals of post-cardiac arrest care are as follows:

- Optimize ventilation and circulation
- Preserve heart function
- Preserve brain function
- Maintain optimal blood glucose levels

ALGORITHM 3: POST-CARDIAC ARREST CARE ALGORITHM

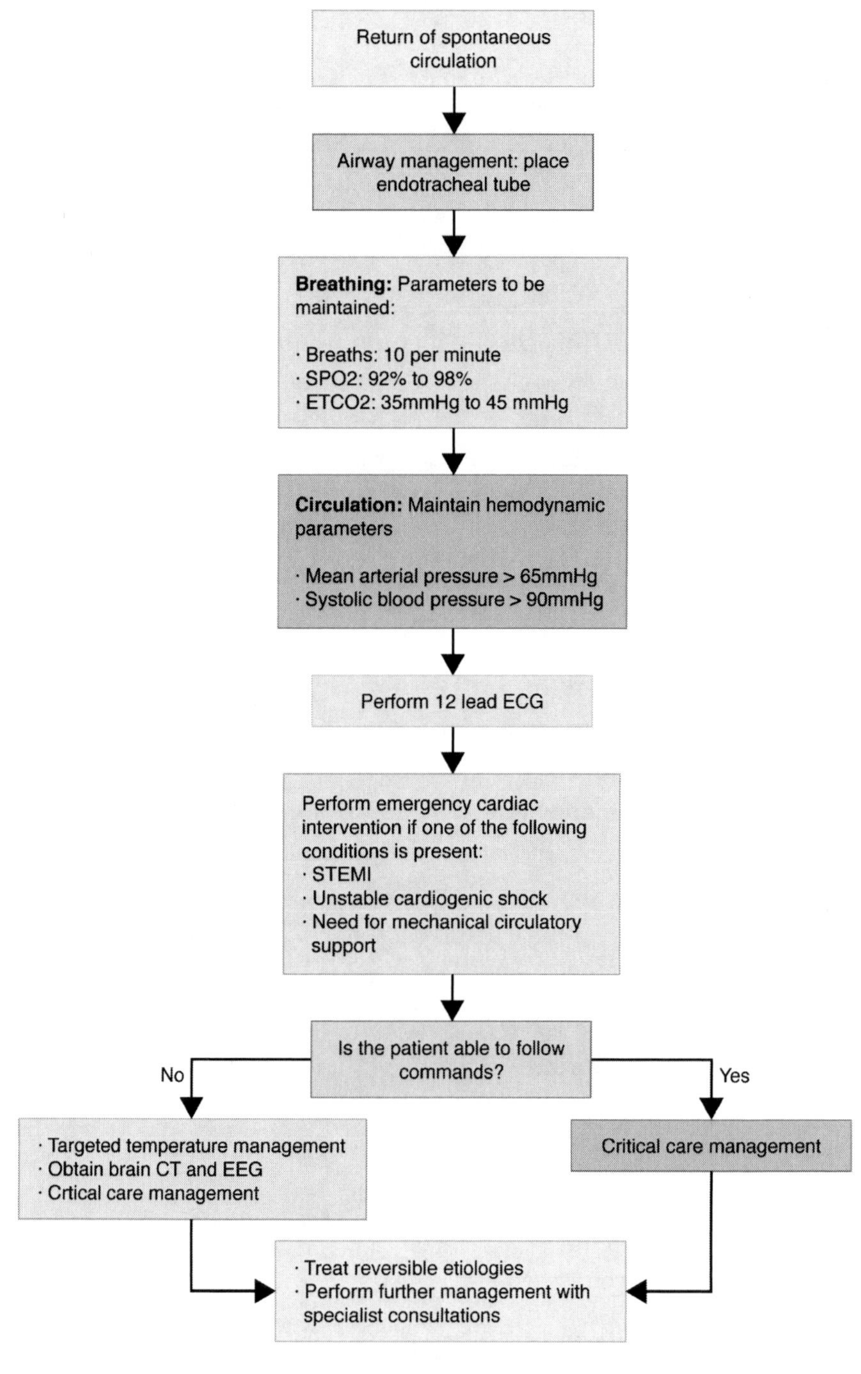

Post-cardiac arrest care, like the ACLS algorithm, must pay attention to airway, breathing, and circulation in turn.

MANAGEMENT OF AIRWAY AND BREATHING:

- If an ET tube was not placed prior to ROSC, it may be placed now. Continue to monitor perfusion using waveform capnography.
- Avoiding hypoxia in the post-cardiac arrest period is a high priority. Therefore, the highest available concentration of oxygen must be delivered to the patient (preferably 100%), and SpO2 levels must be maintained between 92% to 98%.
- Arterial blood gases must be obtained to evaluate for hypoxia and acidosis. Thereafter, titrate oxygen to maintain PaCO2 levels between 35mmHg and 45 mmHg.

MANAGEMENT OF CIRCULATION:

Blood pressure support:

- This should be provided if the patient has systolic blood pressure less than 90mmHg, or a mean arterial pressure less than 65mmHg.
- Initially, provide 1-2 liters of intravenous fluids, such as 0.9% normal saline or lactated Ringer's solution.
- If there is no improvement, the use of vasopressors must be considered.
- The first choice of vasopressor is epinephrine. Other alternatives include dopamine, methoxamine, or phenylephrine. Norepinephrine is usually not preferred unless there is severe hypotension.
- Vasopressors are usually given as infusions. The infusion rate must be titrated according to the blood pressure values to maintain optimum pressure. Standard infusion rates used are:
    - Epinephrine: 0.1 – 0.5 mcg/kg/min
    - Dopamine: 5 – 10 mcg/kg/min
    - Norepinephrine: 0.1 – 0.5 mcg/kg/min

CONSIDER CARDIAC INTERVENTIONS:

- A 12-lead ECG must be obtained for all post-arrest patients. This helps to identify cardiac causes of arrest, and determines the need for cardiac interventions.
- Coronary angiography must be considered if a cardiac cause is strongly suspected, and if STEMI (ST-segment elevated myocardial infarction) is detected. Any block detected during angiography must be resolved with PCI (percutaneous coronary intervention).
- If ST-segment elevation is not detectable on ECG, but the patient is comatose and a cardiac cause is strongly suspected, it may still be reasonable to perform an emergent coronary angiography.
- Irrespective of the state of consciousness, if there are other indications for coronary angiography, (such as a history of chest pain, congenital heart disease, or vascular problems), it must be performed.

TARGETED TEMPERATURE MANAGEMENT (TTM):

- Cardiac arrest is a condition where the whole body essentially goes into ischemia; ROSC restores perfusion. Like other cases of ischemia, there is a chance for reperfusion injury to develop. This involves cell apoptosis, which on a large scale can lead to multiorgan dysfunction. Reperfusion injury is a temperature-sensitive process. It has been shown that hypothermia can slow down or even abort these processes, and can ultimately protect the brain and the heart.
- Targeted temperature management (TTM), also known as mild therapeutic hypothermia, is a process where hypothermia is induced in a patient who has just survived a cardiac arrest.
- In TTM, the patient's body temperature is maintained at a constant temperature between 32°C to 36°C. After the constant temperature is attained, it must be maintained for at least 24 hours.
- In their 2020 guidelines, the AHA recommends TTM for all patients who survive cardiac arrest, regardless of whether it is out-of-hospital or in-hospital, and rhythm type.

- TTM is particularly important in comatose patients, and it is important to prevent fever in this group so that the temperature can be maintained.
- While TTM is advocated after arrest, it must be performed only in the hospital setting. The AHA does not recommend pre-hospital cooling of patients by rapid infusion of cold IV fluids.

MANAGEMENT OF SEIZURES:

- In the post-cardiac arrest period, any clinically apparent seizures that occur must be treated with standard anticonvulsant medication.
- Post-cardiac arrest patients may also be subject to non-convulsive seizures. Therefore, it is good practice to obtain an electroencephalogram (EEG) for all comatose patients to detect such seizures. If non-convulsive seizures are definitely diagnosed, they may be treated.
- If there is no diagnosis of seizures, seizure prophylaxis is not recommended.

CONSIDER OTHER FORMS OF DEFINITIVE MANAGEMENT:

- Certain other forms of management may be considered, given the specific clinical situation and after consultation with experts. However, they all have uncertain benefit in literature.
- Maintaining blood glucose levels within specific target ranges: Insulin may be used to maintain blood glucose levels within a range of 150 to 180mg/dl.
- Use of prophylactic antibiotics: Prophylactic antibiotics may reduce the incidence of nosocomial infections and entry site infections.

Use of drugs to decrease neurological injury

- Use of steroids in patients with shock: Steroids may improve survival in patients with septic shock.

NEUROPROGNOSTICATION:

Neuroprognostication is the process of identifying patients who would have poor neurological outcomes after cardiac arrest. In cardiac arrest, the first organ to be affected by hypoxic-ischemic injury is the brain. As a result, a large number of post-cardiac arrest patients develop poor neurological outcomes. Several times, the cause of death following post-cardiac arrest brain injury is due to active withdrawal of life support treatment, which is based on a prognosis of predicted poor neurological outcome. The decision to withdraw such life support is an important one, and must be made after careful prognostication of neurological factors. A comprehensive neuroprognostication process can also help make informed decisions to the level of care that must be provided to post-cardiac arrest patients.

The AHA therefore makes the following recommendations for proper neuroprognostication:

- Neuroprognostication is essential for all patients who remain comatose after cardiac arrest.
- This process should be multimodal and not based on any one single finding.
- The timing of neuroprognostication is important. If performed too early, there is a risk of confounding because of effect of medications or other factors. Ideally, the multimodal process must be performed at least 72 hours after the patient has attained normothermia. However, any individual prognostic tests may be obtained beforehand.

The various factors that must be considered in the neuroprognostication process are summarized in the diagram below:

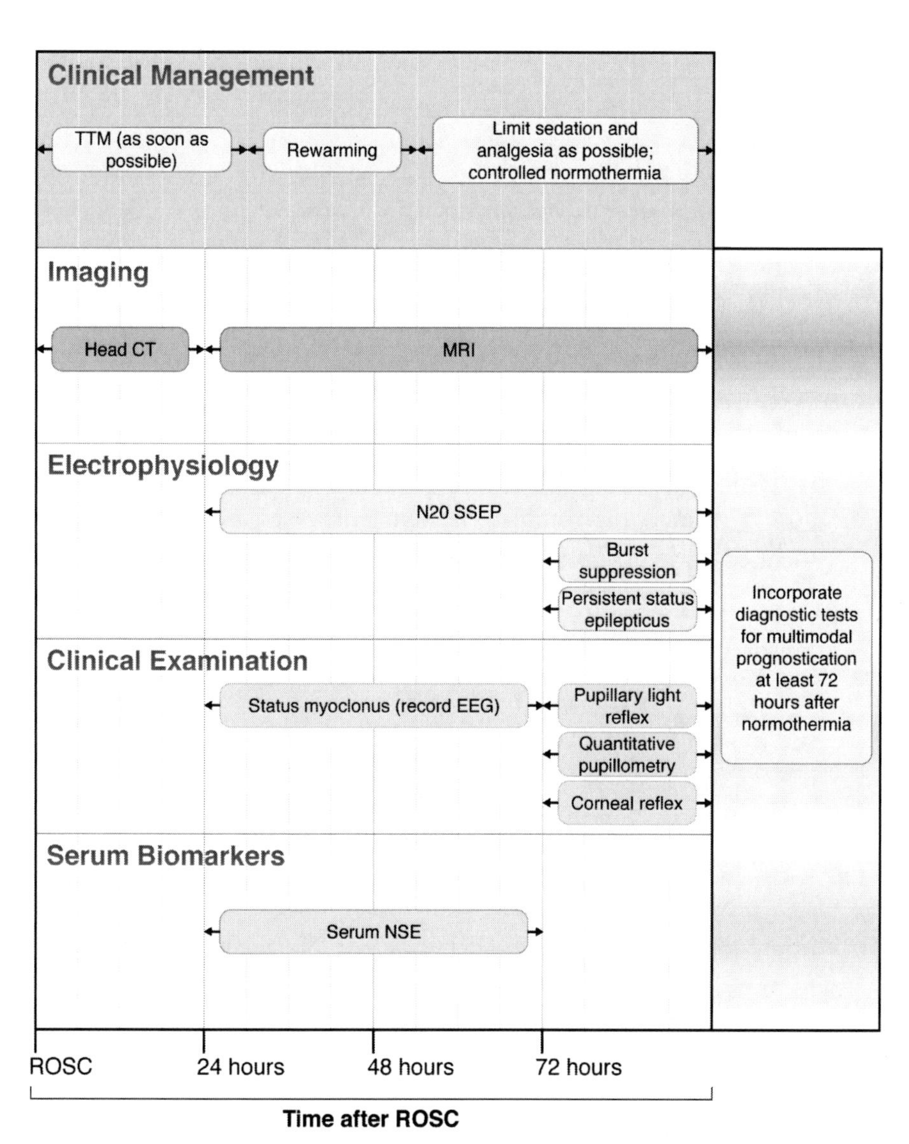

Figure 20. Factors to be taken into account during neuroprognostication

Clinical examination:

On clinical examinations, the following factors must be taken into account. For both clinical and other types of examinations, no single factor can determine prognosis, therefore, all must be taken together into consideration.

- In a comatose patient, absence of bilateral pupillary light reflex more than 72 hours after cardiac arrest is indicative of poor neurological outcomes.
- Absence of bilateral corneal reflexes in comatose patients also indicate poor prognosis.
- Status myoclonus that occurs 72 hours after cardiac arrest supports poor neurological outcomes. When myoclonus occurs, an EEG may be performed to determine if a cerebral correlate is present. Undifferentiated myoclonic movements, however, are not necessarily associated with a poor prognosis.
- Absence of 'best motor response', as per the Glasgow coma scale, or extensor movements alone should not be used to determine prognosis.

Serum biomarkers:

- High serum values of the biomarker neuron-specific enolase (NSE) may be indicative of poor neurological outcomes, when considered along with other factors.
- Other biomarkers have been studied, including the S-100 calcium-binding protein, neurofilament light chain, Tau, and glial fibrillary acid protein. However, at present, their reliability is uncertain.

Electrophysiological tests:

- Routine EEG is usually performed to evaluate the level of electric activity in the brain, and determine the presence of seizures.
- The absence of EEG activity for 72 hours after arrest alone cannot be used as a prognostic indicator. However, when considered along with other tests, the bilateral absence of N-20 somatosensory evoked

potential waves, more than 24 hours after cardiac arrest, could indicate poor neurological outcomes.

- The prognostic value of seizures is uncertain. However, persistent status epilepticus 72 hours after cardiac arrest indicates poor neurological prognosis. Burst suppression on the EEG, 72 hours after cardiac arrest, in the absence of sedating drugs would also indicate poor neurological prognosis.

Neuroimaging studies:

- In brain CT scans, reduced grey:white ratio after cardiac arrest may be indicative of poor neurological outcomes.
- MRI scans may be performed 2 to 7 days after cardiac arrest. Extensive areas of restricted diffusion, and extensive areas of reduced apparent diffusion coefficient may be indicative of poor neurological outcomes.

QUESTIONS

1. Which vasopressor is the first choice in the post-cardiac arrest period, to maintain circulatory support?
   a. Epinephrine
   b. Norepinephrine
   c. Dopamine
   d. Phenylephrine

2. In Targeted temperature management, which of the following tange of core temperatures must be maintained?
   a. 22 to 26 degrees
   b. 26 to 30 degrees
   c. 32 to 36 degrees
   d. 36 to 40 degrees

3. Which of the following parameters is not an indicator of poor neurological outcome?
   a. Status myoclonus
   b. Extensor response to motor stimulus
   c. Absence of bilateral pupillary reflex
   d. Reduced grey white ratio on the CT scan

UNIT VI : MANAGEMENT OF SPECIFIC CASE SCENARIOS

CHAPTER 1

Identification and Management of Non-Arrest Rhythms

Within the hospital setting, the first step of the ACLS chain is prevention of cardiac arrest, which is where the rapid response team comes in. Several times, an abnormal rhythm can be identified on the monitor that may require specific interventions to prevent impending arrest. Similarly, such rhythms may be common in the post-arrest period and may require targeted management.

TORSADES DE POINTES:

This is a condition where there is polymorphic ventricular tachycardia. The ventricular rhythm is disrupted as compared to the atrial rhythm. It can be caused by adverse drug reactions, electrolyte imbalances, or congenital heart syndromes.

ECG findings:

- Rhythm: The rhythm is irregular.
- Rate: Ventricular rate is between 150 and 250 beats per minute. The atrial rate cannot be determined as P waves are absent.
- Waves: The P wave is absent and may be buried in the QRS complex, hence PR interval cannot be identified. The QRS complex is wide and polarity varies; some complexes may be pointed downwards. T waves cannot be identified and QT interval is prolonged.

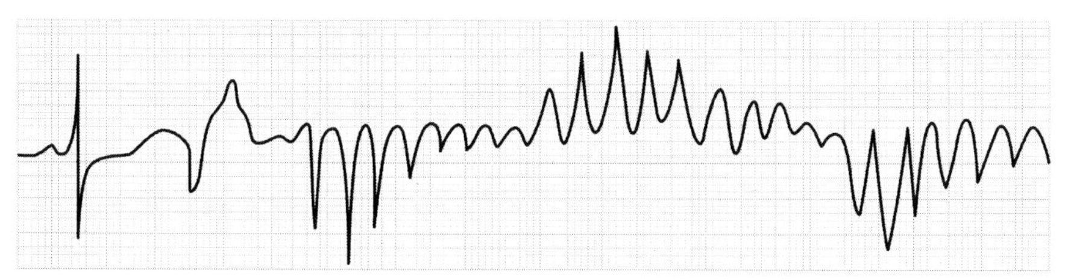

Figure 21. Torsades de pointes

Management:

- Assess the patient's hemodynamic stability.
- If the patient is unstable, immediate defibrillation is recommended. As synchronization is not reliable. If the patient transitions into arrest in front of the rescuer, apply defibrillation immediately and carry out ACLS protocols.
- If the patient is hemodynamically stable, a 12-lead ECG must be obtained to get a precise diagnosis. Anti-arrythmic drugs such as amiodarone, procainamide, or sotalol may be considered. Verapamil and adenosine are not advised for polymorphic tachyarrythmias. Intravenous magnesium may be considered.
- Address the cause: Discontinue offending drugs, correct electrolyte imbalances.
- Consider surgery to place a pacemaker or implantable defibrillator depending on the severity of the condition.

SYMPTOMATIC BRADYCARDIA:

Bradycardia, which is defined as a heart rate of less than 60 beats per minute, is not necessarily a pathological condition. Several healthy people, such as athletes, may have physiological bradycardia. However, if bradycardia occurs due to a pathological entity, the patient may experience certain symptoms, including lightheadedness, dizziness, mental confusion, shortness of breath, or even loss of consciousness. The pathophysiology and common causes of bradycardia are outlined in table 2. In such cases, an ACLS survey must be performed, and the ECG rhythm must be analyzed.

ECG findings:

Several different conditions may present as bradycardia, and these may be differentiated on the ECG.

Sinus bradycardia:

- Rhythm: The overall rhythm is regular.
- Rate: Usually between 40 to 60 beats per minute.
- Waves: The waves appear normal. PR interval is normal and consistent.

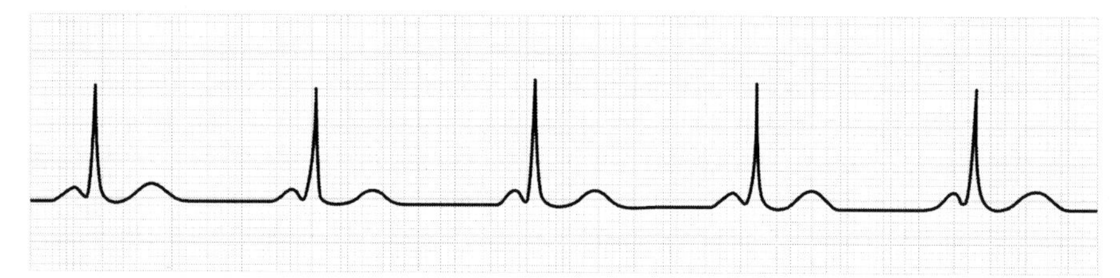

Figure 22. Sinus bradycardia

First-degree AV block:

- Rhythm: The overall rhythm is regular.
- Rate: Atrial and ventricular rates are the same and within normal range.
- Waves: P waves appear normal. PR interval is prolonged, QRS complex is narrow.

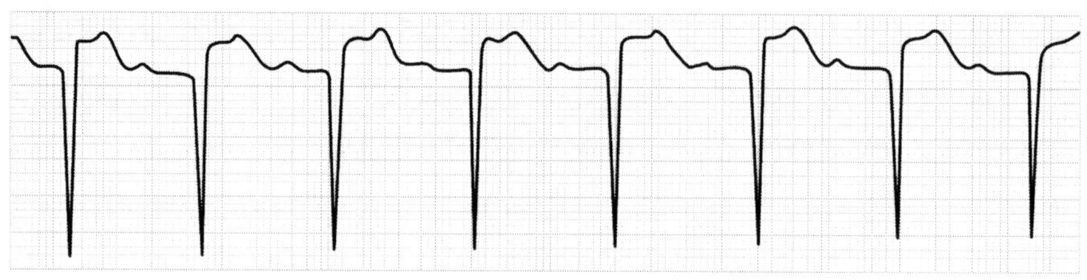

Figure 23. First degree AV block

Second-degree AV block – type I:

- Rhythm: The atrial rhythm is regular while the ventricular rhythm may be irregular.
- Rate: Usually between 40 to 60 beats per minute, but the atrial rate appears to be faster than the ventricular rate.
- Waves: P waves appear normal, but occasionally may not be followed by a QRS complex. PR interval progressively lengthens between each cycle until the QRS complex disappears altogether for one cycle.

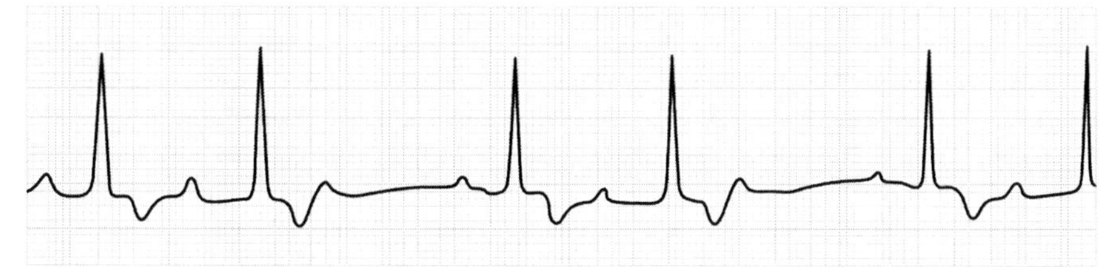

Figure 24. Second degree AV block - Type I

Second degree AV block – type II:

- Rhythm: Atrial rhythm is regular; ventricular rhythm may either be irregular, or regular with a 2:1 or 3:1 block.
- Rate: Atrial rate is usually between 60 to 100 beats per minute; ventricular rate is slower.
- Waves: P waves and PR intervals are normal. QRS complexes are narrow; some QRS complexes are absent or 'dropped'.

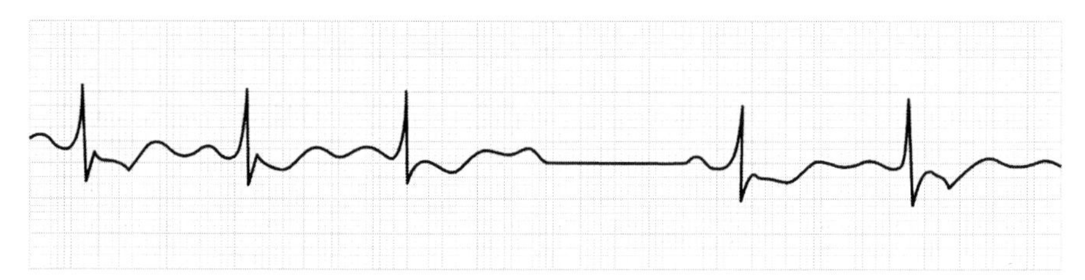

Figure 25. Second degree AV block Type II

Third-degree AV block:

- Rhythm: Both the atrial and ventricular rhythms are regular but differ from each other.
- Rate: Atrial and ventricular rates are completely dissociated. The atrial rate is usually 60 to 100 beats per minute. The ventricular rate depends on the number of escape beats. If the escape bears are slow, VR may be 20 to 40 beats per minute, whereas if the escape beats are fast, the VR may be 40 to 55 beats per minute.
- Waves: The waves appear normal. PR interval is normal and consistent.

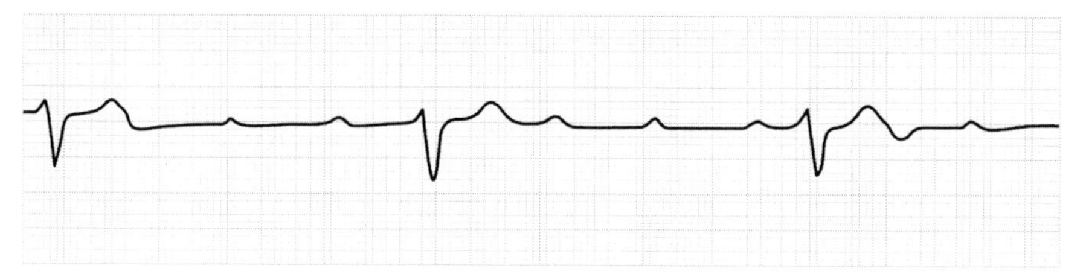

Figure 26. Third degree AV block

Table 2. Pathophysiology and causes of symptomatic bradycardia

RHYTHM	PATHOPHYSIOLOGY	COMMON ETIOLOGICAL FACTORS
Sinus bradycardia	Origin of impulses at SA node slows down	Vasovagal syncope, pressure on carotid sinus, valsalva maneuver
First degree AV block	Block is at or before AV node: Conduction of impulses to the AV node is slowed down	Drugs: beta blockers, calcium channel blockers, digoxin Vasovagal reflexes Acute myocardial infarction

Second-degree AV block - type I (Mobitz I - Wenckebach block)	Block is within the AV node: Conduction of impulses at the AV node is slowed down	Drugs: beta blockers, calcium channel blockers, digoxin Acute coronary syndrome of the right coronary artery Parasympathetic nervous system stimulation
Second-degree AV block - type II	Block is below the AV node, usually at the Bundle of His or bundle branches	Acute coronary syndrome of the left coronary artery.
Third-degree AV block	Referred to as complete AV block or AV dissociation; no impulses pass between the atria and ventricles. This block can occur at the level of the AV node, bundle of His, or bundle branches.	Acute coronary syndrome of the left coronary artery - usually the left anterior descending artery and branches to the interventricular septum.

Management of symptomatic bradycardia:

- If a patient presents with symptomatic bradycardia, the cause must be ascertained and addressed.
- Hemodynamic status must be evaluated. If there is hemodynamic compromise, atropine may be administered to increase the heart rate.
- If the bradycardia does not respond to atropine:
- A rate accelerating agent, such as epinephrine may be administered.
- Alternatively, transcutaneous pacing can be considered.
- Patient can be prepared for emergent transvenous pacing.
- If IV/IO access is not available, and the patient is unstable (e.g., a high-degree AV block), immediate pacing should be carried out.

The following algorithm may be followed for comprehensive management of symptomatic bradycardia:

ALGORITHM 4: MANAGEMENT OF SYMPTOMATIC BRADYCARDIA IN ADULTS

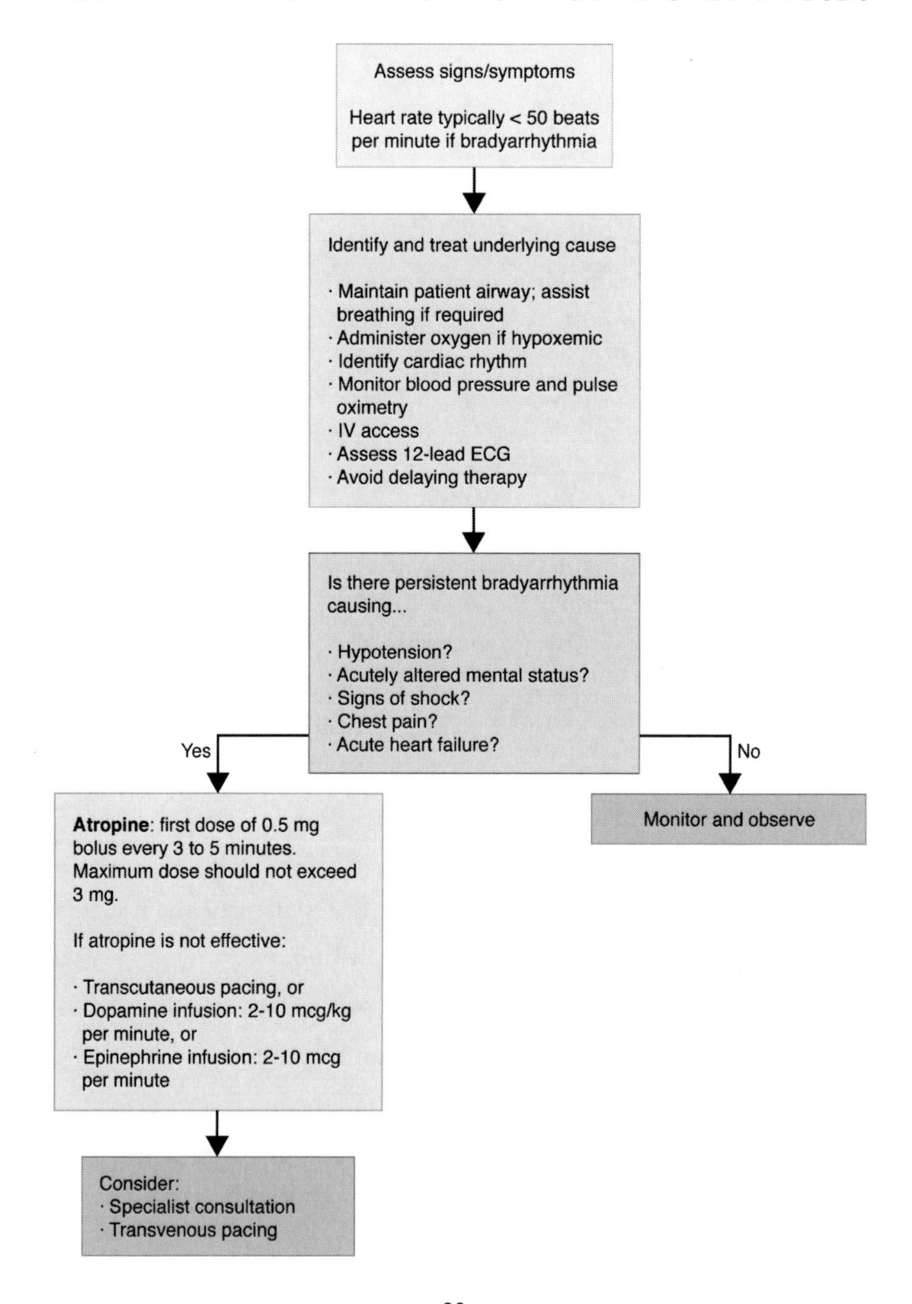

SYMPTOMATIC TACHYCARDIA:

A heart rate of greater than 100 beats per minute is usually referred to as tachycardia. Tachycardia may be stable or unstable, and symptoms may occur if the heart rate crosses 150 beats per minute. This may be felt as a bounding pulse, flutters, shortness of breath, and chest tightness or pain. There may also be some degree of lightheadedness and altered mental state.

ECG rhythms in tachycardia:

Sinus tachycardia:

- Rhythm: Rhythm is normal.
- Rate: Usually above 100 beats per minute.
- Waves: P waves and PR intervals are normal. QRS complexes may either be normal or wide in case of an underlying abnormality.

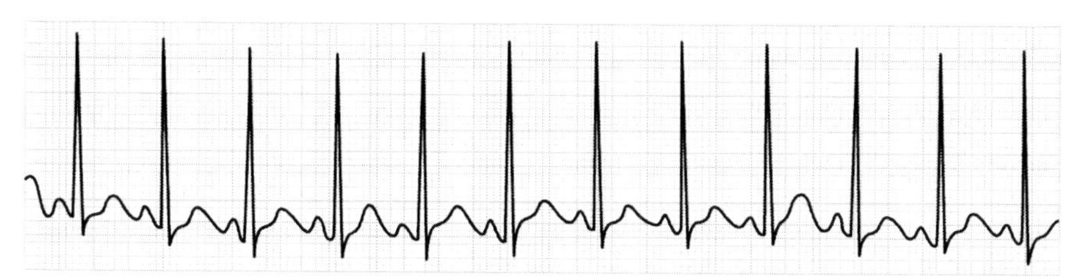

Figure 27. Sinus tachycardia

Atrial fibrillation:

- Rhythm: Rhythm is irregularly irregular.
- Rate: May range from 300 to 400 beats per minute.
- Waves: Chaotic P waves are seen. PR interval is absent. QRS complexes are usually normal, but may sometimes be distorted.

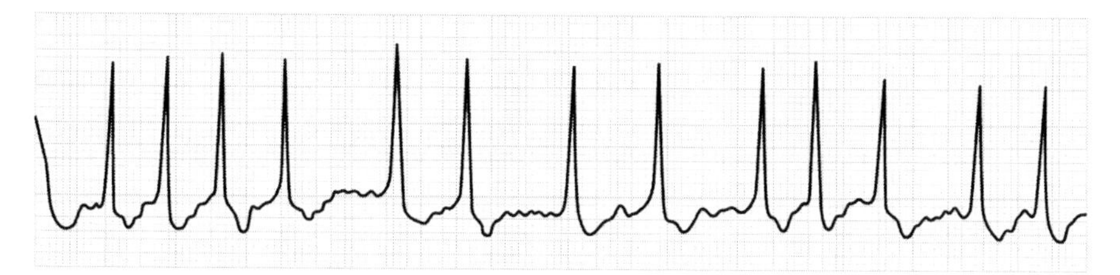

Figure 28. Atrial fibrillation

Atrial flutter:

- Rhythm: Usually regular, ventricular rhythm may have a 2:1 or 4:1 ratio to atrial rhythm.
- Rate: Atrial rate may range from 220 to 350 beats per minute. Ventricular rate is usually 150 to 180 beats per minute.
- Waves: True P waves are absent. A 'sawtooth' pattern of flutter waves is seen. PR interval is absent. QRS complexes are usually normal, but may sometimes be distorted.

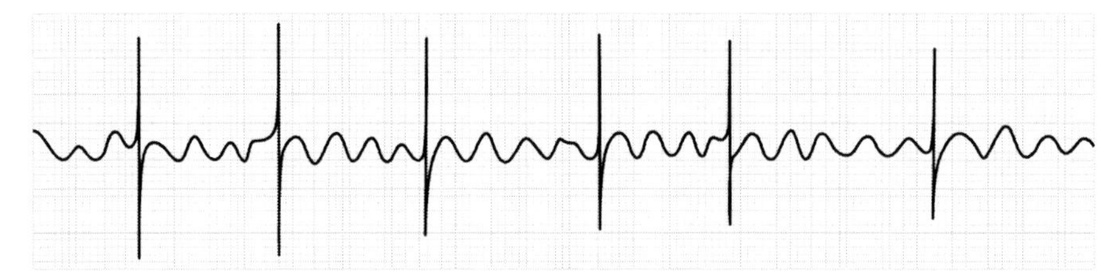

Figure 29. Atrial flutter

Supraventricular tachycardia (AV reentry tachycardia):

- Rhythm: Rhythm is usually regular.
- Rate: Usually very high, ranging from 220 to 250 beats per minute.
- Waves: P waves are present but usually merge with the preceding T waves and cannot be discerned. QRS complexes are normal and narrow.

Monomorphic ventricular tachycardia:

- Rhythm: No atrial rhythm is detected. Ventricular rhythm is usually regular.
- Rate: Ventricular rate is high; can range from 120 to 250 beats per minute.
- Waves: P waves are present but cannot be discerned. PR interval is absent. QRS complexes have a bizzare, wide appearance. Fusion beats may occur.

Figure 30. Monomorphic ventricular tachycardia

Polymorphic ventricular tachycardia:

- Rhythm: No atrial rhythm is detected; ventricular rhythm may be regular or irregular.
- Rate: Ventricular rate is high; can range from 120 to 250 beats per minute.
- Waves: P waves are present but cannot be discerned. PR interval is absent. QRS complexes are variable and inconsistent.

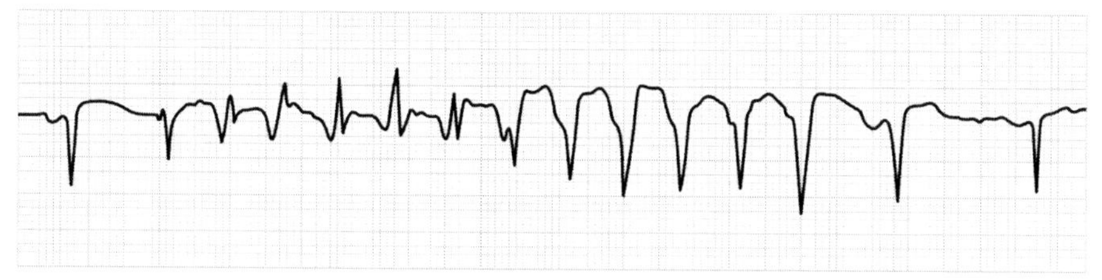

Figure 31. Polymorphic ventricular tachycardia

Table 3. Pathophysiology and causes of symptomatic tachycardia

RHYTHM	PATHOPHYSIOLOGY	COMMON ETIOLOGICAL FACTORS
Sinus tachycardia	Usually a normal physiological response; SA node generates impulses faster than usual.	Fever, anemia, hyperthyroidism, pain, anxiety.

Atrial fibrillation	Occurs when impulse conduction through atrium is faster than impulse generation through AV node. Impulses are transmitted through the atria via multiple, random, chaotic pathways.	Acute coronary syndromes Hyperthyroidism Valvular heart disease Hypertension Pulmonary embolism Drug-induced: digoxin, theophylline
Atrial flutter	Occurs when impulse conduction through atrium is faster than impulse generation through AV node. Impulses are conducted in a circular course around the atria.	Same as for atrial fibrillation.
Supraventricular tachycardia	Due to abnormal rhythm circuit, impulses recycle in the AV node; allowing impulses to propagate through normal as well as abnormal pathways.	Coronary artery disease, chronic obstructive pulmonary disease, congestive heart failure
Monomorphic ventricular tachycardia	There are areas of ventricular injury, at which conduction is slowed. These injured areas can also generate ectopic impulses.	Acute ischemic event Chronic heart failure causing low ejection fraction Drugs: procainamide, tricyclic antidepressants, antipsychotics, antihistamines)
Polymorphic ventricular tachycardia	There are areas of ventricular injury, at which conduction is slowed. These injured areas can also generate ectopic impulses.	Drugs: procainamide, tricyclic antidepressants, antipsychotics, antihistamines) Acute ischemic episodes Hereditary syndromes

Management of atrial fibrillation/flutter:

- Patients who are hemodynamically unstable, who have rapid ventricular response, should undergo electric cardioversion.
- If the cause of atrial fibrillation is acute coronary syndrome, and the patient exhibits hemodynamic compromise, ongoing ischemia, or inadequate rate control, urgent cardioversion must be considered.
- If a biphasic defibrillator is used, the optimal energy setting for synchronized cardioversion is 120 to 200 J for atrial fibrillation, and is 50 to 100 J for atrial flutter.
- If the patient is hemodynamically stable, and there is rapid ventricular response without pre-excitation, a beta-adrenergic blocker or a non-dihydropyridine calcium channel antagonist may be administered intravenously. These drugs must not be used in patients who have decompensated heart failure and left ventricular systolic dysfunction, as the hemodynamic compromise may be further accentuated.
- Amiodarone is also useful for rate control, particularly in critically ill patients.
- If there is pre-excitation, the above drugs and digoxin should not be used, as they can further increase the ventricular response, which can result in ventricular fibrillation.

Management of symptomatic ventricular tachycardia:

The management of symptomatic ventricular tachycardia usually depends on the kind of QRS complex present. Based on this, the tachycardias are categorized as wide complex and narrow complex tachycardias.

Wide complex tachycardias:

- If the patient is hemodynamically stable, and the cause is not immediately identifiable, IV adenosine may be administered. However, this drug must be avoided in hemodynamically unstable cases.

- Other drugs that may be administered include IV amiodarone, procainamide, and sotalol.
- Unless the tachycardia is definitely known to be of supraventricular origin, administration of verapamil is not recommended.
- In hemodynamically stable patients, if pharmacological therapy is unsuccessful, expert consultation must be sought, and cardioversion must be considered.

Narrow complex tachycardias:

- If patients are hemodynamically unstable, synchronized cardioversion is immediately recommended.
- In patients who are hemodynamically stable, pharmacological therapy may be attempted first, in combination with vagal maneuvers.
- For patients with SVT, adenosine is recommended. However, IV diltiazem or verapamil can also be effective. IV beta adrenergic blockers may also be reasonably considered.
- For vagal maneuvers, the valsalva maneuver is the most effective. This may be augmented with a passive leg raise to make it more effective. Carotid massage must be employed with caution, as it carries the risk of thromboembolism.
- If both pharmacological treatment and vagal maneuvers are unsuccessful, synchronized cardioversion is recommended.

A comprehensive algorithm for the management of symptomatic tachycardia is detailed below.

ALGORITHM 5: MANAGEMENT OF SYMPTOMATIC TACHYCARDIA

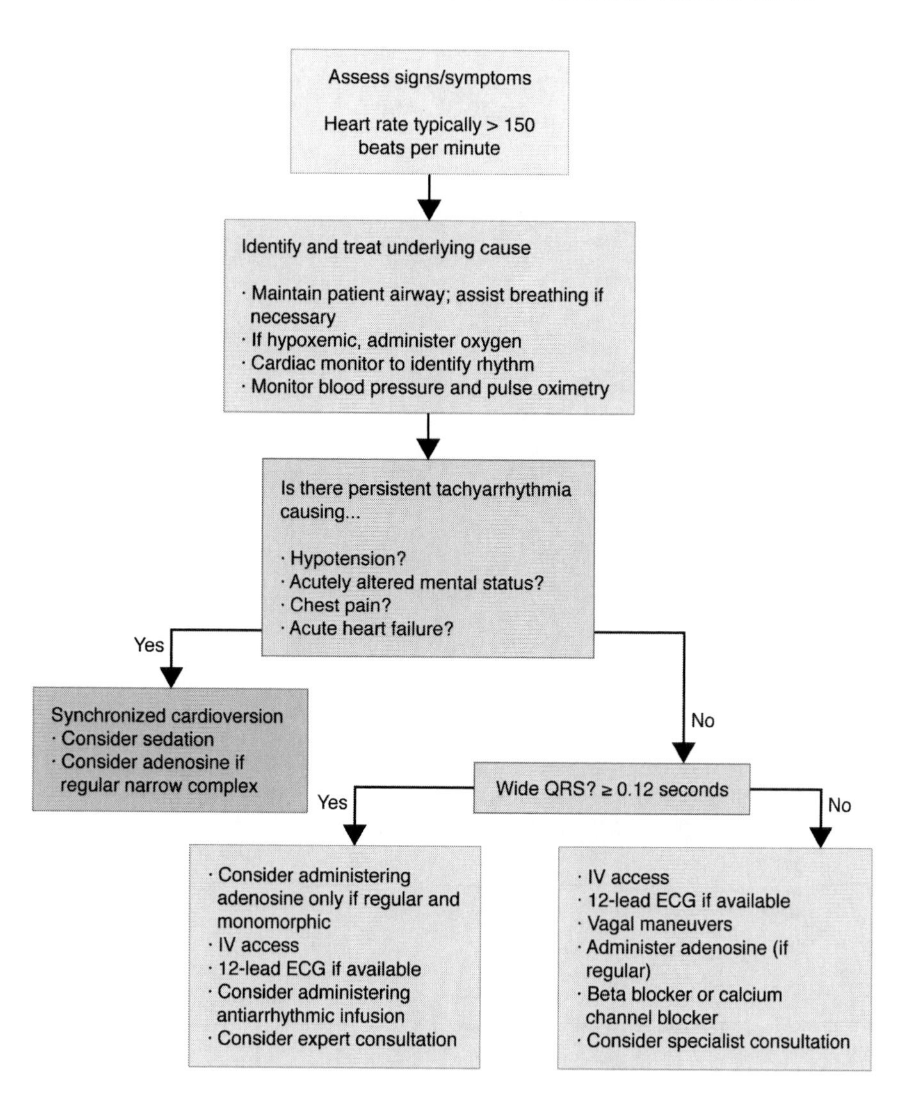

QUESTIONS

1. Which of the following abnormal rhythms requires immediate defibrillation if hemodynamically unstable?
   a. First degree AV block
   b. Monomorphic ventricular tachycardia
   c. Supraventricular tachycardia
   d. Torsades de Pointes

2. Which of the following rhythms consists of a 'dropped' QRS complex?
   a. First degree AV block
   b. Second degree AV block type I
   c. Second degree AV block type II
   d. Third degree AV block

3. Which of the following may be used to treat symptomatic bradycardia
   a. Atropine
   b. Epinephrine
   c. Transcutaneous pacing
   d. All of the above

4. Vagal maneuver is useful in which of the following abnormal rhythms?
   a. Atrial fibrillation
   b. Ventricular fibrillation
   c. Wide complex tachycardia
   d. Narrow complex tachycardia

CHAPTER 2

Management of Opioid Emergencies

KEY 2020 GUIDELINE UPDATES

The AHA has issued a new algorithm for management of suspected opioid overdose by ACLS providers.

Both lay rescuers and ACLS providers must receive specific training for handling emergencies related to opioid overdose.

Pediatric opioid overdose: While focus should be on providing high-quality CPR plus ventilation, however, administration of naloxone by responders is reasonable.

The increase in misuse of prescription as well as non-prescription opioids in the recent years has led to what is now known as the 'opioid epidemic'. This epidemic has been known to primarily target patients between 25 and 65 years of age, and is said to be responsible for at least 115 deaths per day. Opioid overdoses primarily cause depression of the respiratory system and central nervous system, leading to respiratory arrest. If this is left untreated, it can progress to cardiac arrest.

One of the main reasons that opioid emergencies have been highlighted in the 2020 guidelines is due to the shift in priorities during resuscitation. In normal circumstances, focus is first given to maintaining circulation.

However, since opioids primarily cause respiratory distress, focus is shifted to maintenance of airway and breathing. The C-A-B-D assessment therefore shifts to an A-B-C-D assessment. Below, we describe the latest algorithm given by the AHA for ACLS care providers to follow when they suspect that the patient is a victim of opioid toxicity.

ALGORITHM 6: ALGORITHM FOR OPIOID EMERGENCIES

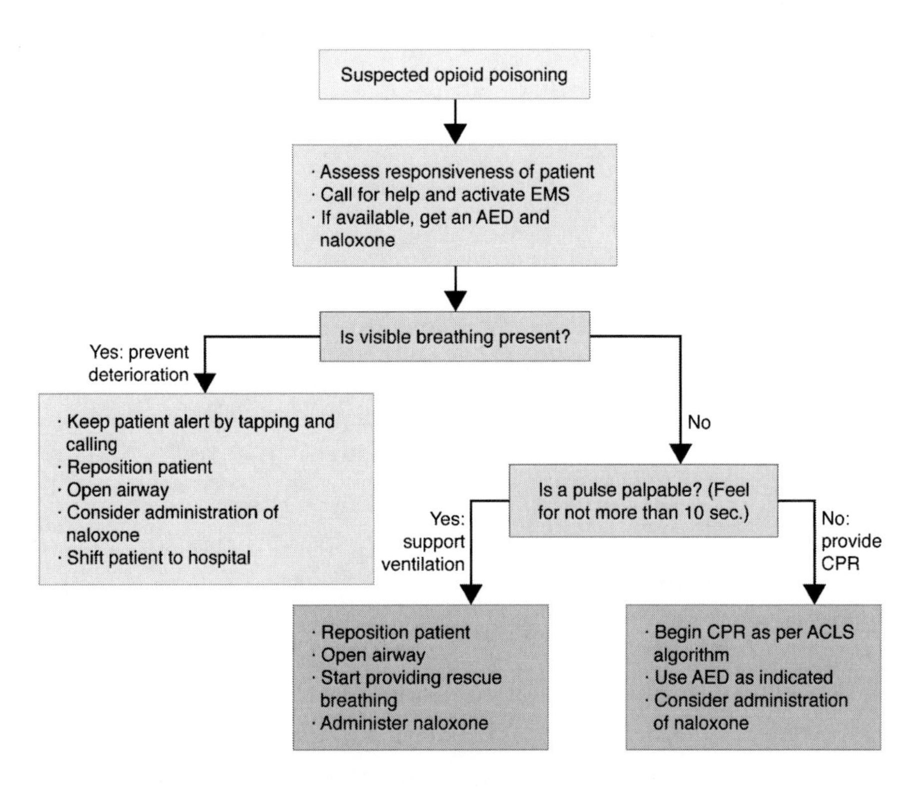

When to suspect an opioid overdose:

- Eyewitness accounts or history of usage from bystanders, family, or friends.
- There is evidence of drug usage paraphernalia – injections or pill bottles.
- Patient exhibits pupillary miosis, or needle tracks on skin

Specific CPR considerations:

- Initially, focus on supporting airway and breathing. This will necessitate opening up the airway and using bag-mask ventilation.
- Focus must remain on delivering high-quality CPR. Naloxone, if administered, should not interfere with the ACLS protocol.
- Trained rescuers may perform both compressions and rescue breathing for adults. Untrained rescuers should perform hands-only CPR.
- For infants and children, both trained and untrained observers must alternate compressions with rescue breathing.

Utility of naloxone in the opioid algorithm:

- Naloxone is an opioid antagonist which works by competitively bonding to opioid receptors. It has been shown to significantly improve prognosis following opioid overdose.
- The U.S. FDA has approved intranasal naloxone for use in emergencies. This is available as a single dose sprayer which delivers 4mg of the drug with a single use. This is yet to be validated as an alternative to the intravenous route.

Post-resuscitation management of opioid overdose:

- Even if spontaneous breathing returns, it is advisable to transport the patient to a hospital setting for monitoring. This is because, even after administration of naloxone, patients may develop recurrent depression of the CNS or respiratory system.
- Some opioids may have longer duration of action as compared to naloxone. If toxicity is due to these drugs, repeated doses, or continuous infusion of naloxone may be necessary.

QUESTIONS

1. Which of the following is the preferred antidote for opioid emergencies?
    a. Pethidine
    b. Naloxone
    c. Oxycodone
    d. Felypressin

2. What is the dose of naloxone that may be administered intranasally?
    a. 2mg
    b. 3mg
    c. 4mg
    d. 5mg

CHAPTER 3

Acute Coronary Syndrome

Acute coronary syndrome (ACS) is an umbrella term that is used to describe a state of sudden, reduced blood flow to the cardiac muscle, which can lead to myocardial ischemia and eventually, necrosis of cardiac muscle. ACS generally encompasses all types of myocardial infarction, (ST-segment elevation MI and non-ST-segment elevation MI), as well as unstable angina. The most common cause is a ruptured atherosclerotic plaque. In the absence of early, definitive management, the patient may develop cardiac arrest.

Signs and symptoms of acute coronary syndrome:

- Crushing chest pain
- Levine's sign: Patient holding a clenched first over chest
- Pain radiating to the left arm, shoulder, lower jaw, and neck
- Profuse sweating
- Shortness of breath
- Nausea or vomiting
- Palpitations

It is important to remember that patients with diabetes and women may not experience the above classic signs. Therefore, it is important to maintain a high degree of suspicion.

Management of ACS:

Early recognition and appropriate management can greatly improve the prognosis of patients who develop ACS. For this reason, the AHA has outlined a special chain of survival for patients in whom symptoms of ACS have been recognized. This is given below:

ALGORITHM 7: CHAIN OF SURVIVAL IN PATIENTS WITH ACUTE CORONARY SYNDROME

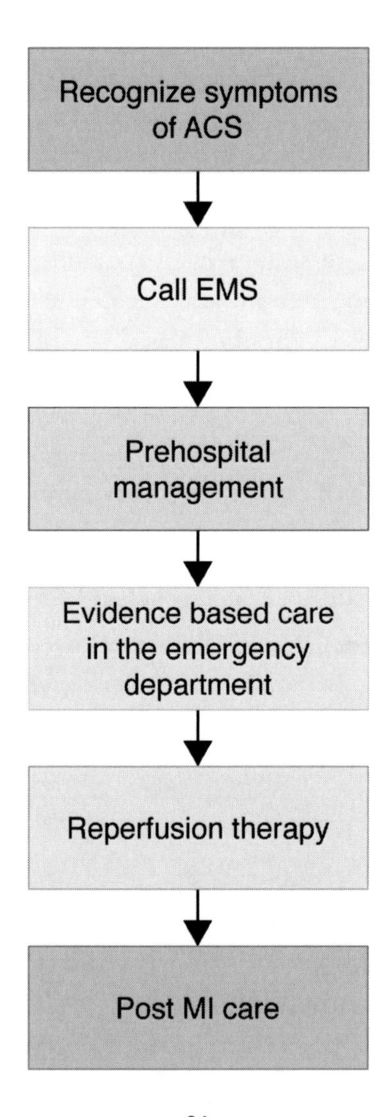

The primary goals of management are to reduce myocardial necrosis in order to preserve cardiac function, treat complications of ACS, including ventricular fibrillation, ventricular tachycardia, and shock, and prevent any major adverse cardiac events.

EMS management of ACS:

- Emergency management of ACS must follow the acronym MONA: Morphine, oxygen, nitroglycerin, and aspirin.
- Oxygen: High flow oxygen may be provided at the rate of 4L/minute. This will help alleviate hypoxic damage to the myocardium.
- Aspirin: If possible, ascertain allergy to aspirin. If the patient is not allergic, 160mg to 325mg of aspirin can be given, to be chewed by the patient. Aspirin is an antiplatelet agent and helps limit the size of the infarct.
- Nitroglycerin: This is a coronary vasodilator and can provide pain relief by improving blood flow to the myocardium. A dose of 0.3 to 0.6 mg may be delivered sublingually. Nitroglycerin must be avoided if the systolic blood pressure is below 90 mmHg, and if the patient has taken phosphodiesterase inhibitors within the last 24 hours.
- Morphine: This must be used if symptoms of pain have not been relieved by use of nitroglycerin, or if symptoms recur. A dose of 1 to 5mg may be administered intravenously.
- Obtain intravenous access: A large IV access, preferably in the antecubital fossa, must be obtained. This can aid in easy delivery of emergency drugs, should the need arise.
- Obtain a 12-lead ECG: As soon as it is available, a 12-lead ECG must be obtained to look for signs of myocardial infarction. ST-segment elevation or depression, and poor progression of R waves are signs that an MI has occurred.
- Once the patient has been shifted to the hospital, definitive management takes over. The AHA has recommended the following algorithm for ACS care in the hospital.

ALGORITHM 8: MANAGEMENT OF ACUTE CORONARY SYNDROME

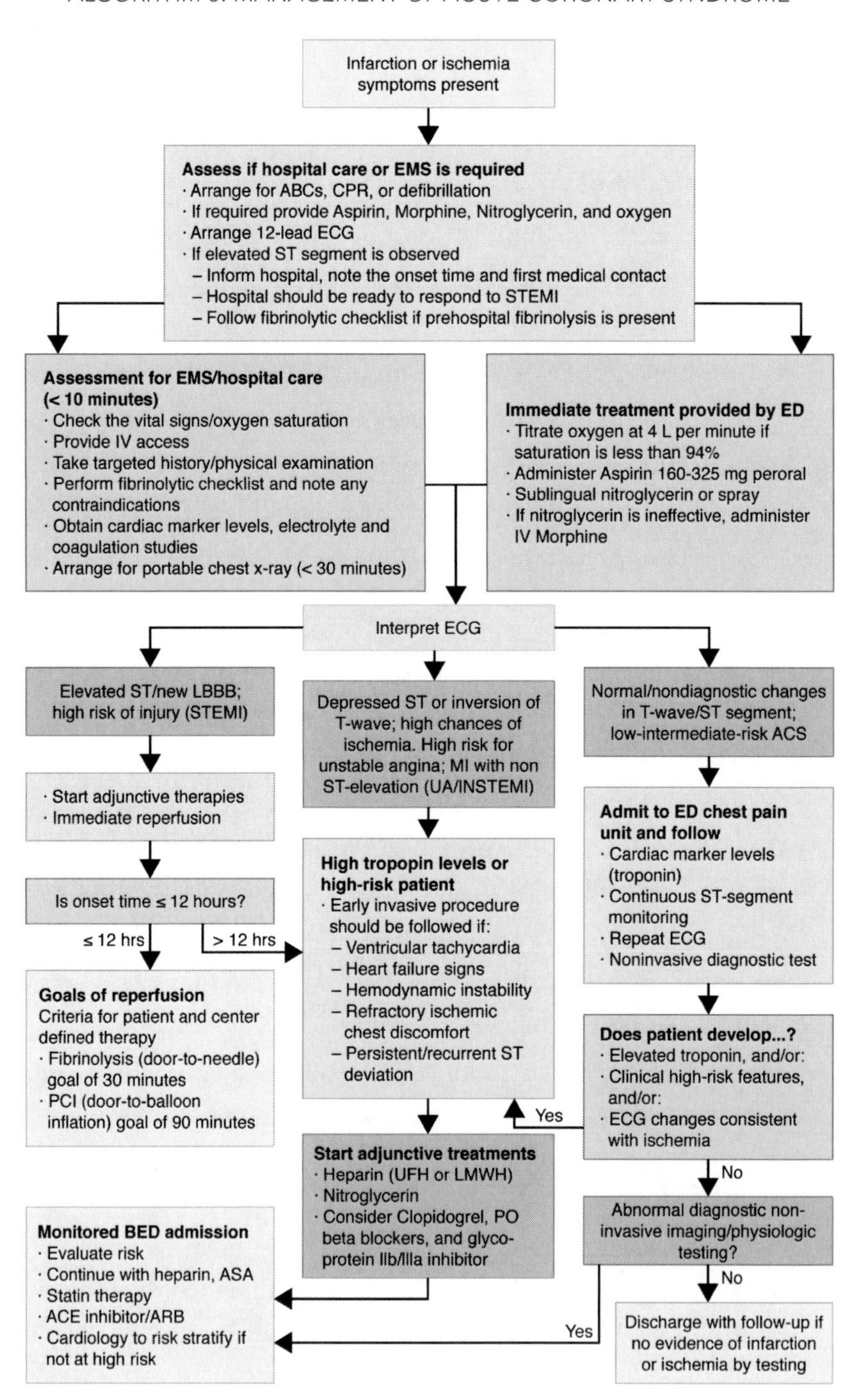

QUESTIONS

1. Which of the following drugs is not part of the emergency management of patients with acute coronary syndrome?

   a. Morphine
   b. Streptokinase
   c. Aspirin
   d. Nitroglycerin

2. Which of the following is a key cardiac marker used to make treatment decisions in ACS?

   a. Creatine phosphokinase
   b. Lactate dehydrogenase
   c. Troponin
   d. Myoglobin

CHAPTER 4

Management of Stroke

Stroke is defined as the sudden loss of blood circulation to a region of the brain. This is broadly classified into ischemic stroke and hemorrhagic stroke. While ischemic stroke is more common, and results from thrombotic occlusion of the cerebral arteries, the less common hemorrhagic stroke can occur because of rupture of a blood vessel.

Symptoms of stroke:

Both ischemic stroke and hemorrhagic stroke present with similar symptoms. These include:

- Weakness in the arm, leg or face; sudden palsy is often the first sign of a stroke.
- Slurred speech; difficulty in speaking and forming words
- Blurred vision or other visual problems
- Severe headache
- Nausea and vomiting

Management of stroke:

Like acute coronary syndrome, the prognosis of stroke improves greatly if prompt treatment is instituted. Therefore, the AHA has put forward a stroke chain of survival:

ALGORITHM 9: CHAIN OF SURVIVAL FOR PATIENTS WITH SUSPECTED STROKE

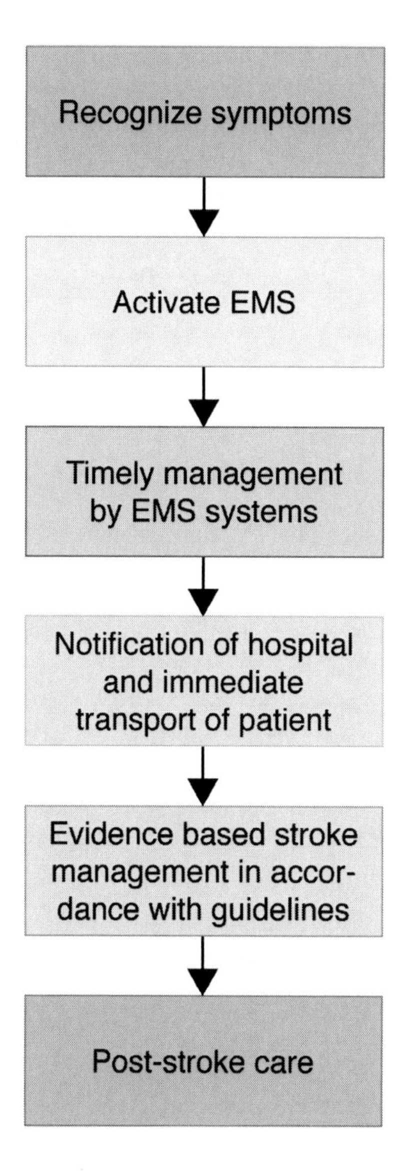

The AHA has determined that delay can occur at several areas during this process, which they refer to as the 8 Ds. These areas, and methods to overcome these delays are outlined below.

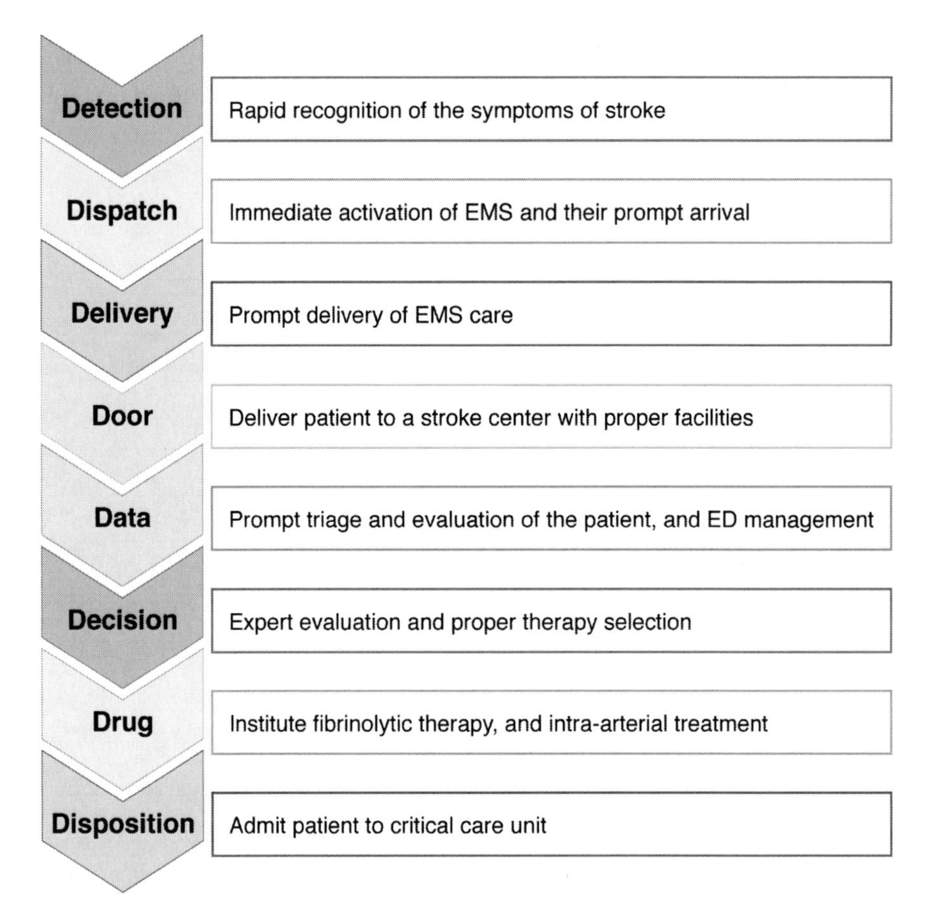

Figure 32. 8 Ds that can affect prognosis in a stroke patient

Management of stroke in out-of-hospital setting:

- Oxygen: Provide 100% oxygen to the patient; titrate oxygen according to the oxygen saturation if possible.
- Capillary blood glucose: Often, hypoglycemia may mimic the symptoms of a stroke. Therefore, the EMS provider can perform a finger stick test to rule this out.
- Obtain patient history: If possible, question bystanders or family members about the time of onset of symptoms.

- Examine for neurological deficits: Perform neurological assessment of all motor nerves, sensory nerves, and cranial nerves, and record any deficits present.
- Institute precautions to keep the patient safe if seizures develop.
- Obtain intravenous access: Preferably, obtain a large bore access in the antecubital fossa. This will be useful for drug delivery.
- Appropriate transport: As far as possible, take the patient to a stroke center which will have the requisite facilities for immediate management.

On arrival in the Emergency Department:

The ED staff should perform a prompt clinical evaluation, obtain a CT scan to confirm diagnosis, and assess the patient for feasibility of fibrinolytic therapy. All the above actions must be performed in a timely manner. The National Institutes of Neurological disorders and stroke (NINDS) have established certain time goals, if the time of symptom onset is definitely known. This is outlined in the figure below.

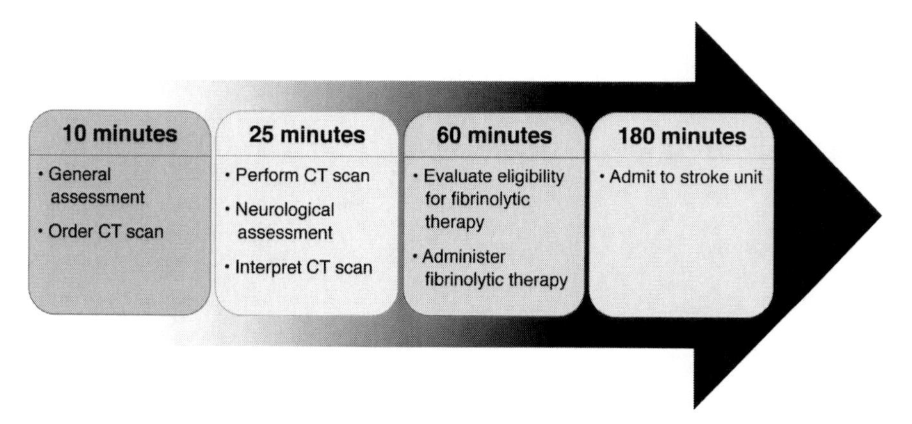

Figure 33. Time bound assessment of stroke patient in the ED

Checklist for fibrinolytic therapy:

Patients may be assessed for the feasibility of fibrinolytic therapy using the following checklist. If these criteria are met, fibrinolytics must not be administered.

INCLUSION CRITERIA	ABSOLUTE EXCLUSION CRITERIA	RELATIVE EXCLUSION CRITERIA
• Onset of symptoms within the last three hours • Patient is 18 years of age or older • Acute ischemic stroke, where neurological deficit is present	• History of head trauma in the last three months. • History of stroke in the last three months • Evidence of intracranial hemorrhage • History of arterial puncture in the last 7 days • Active bleeding • Subarachnoid hemorrhage • Heparin intake in the last two days • Elevated INR • Hypoglycemia • Brain infarct that involves multiple lobes • Thrombocytopenia with platelet count less than 100,000 per micro liter	• Minor stroke with resolving symptoms • Presence of seizures that could potentially affect neurological examinations • Surgery or trauma that occurred in the last 14 days • Major GI or urinary tract bleeding that occurred within the last 21 days • Myocardial infarction that occurred within the last three months

A comprehensive algorithm for the management of stroke is presented below:

ALGORITHM 10: MANAGEMENT OF ACUTE STROKE

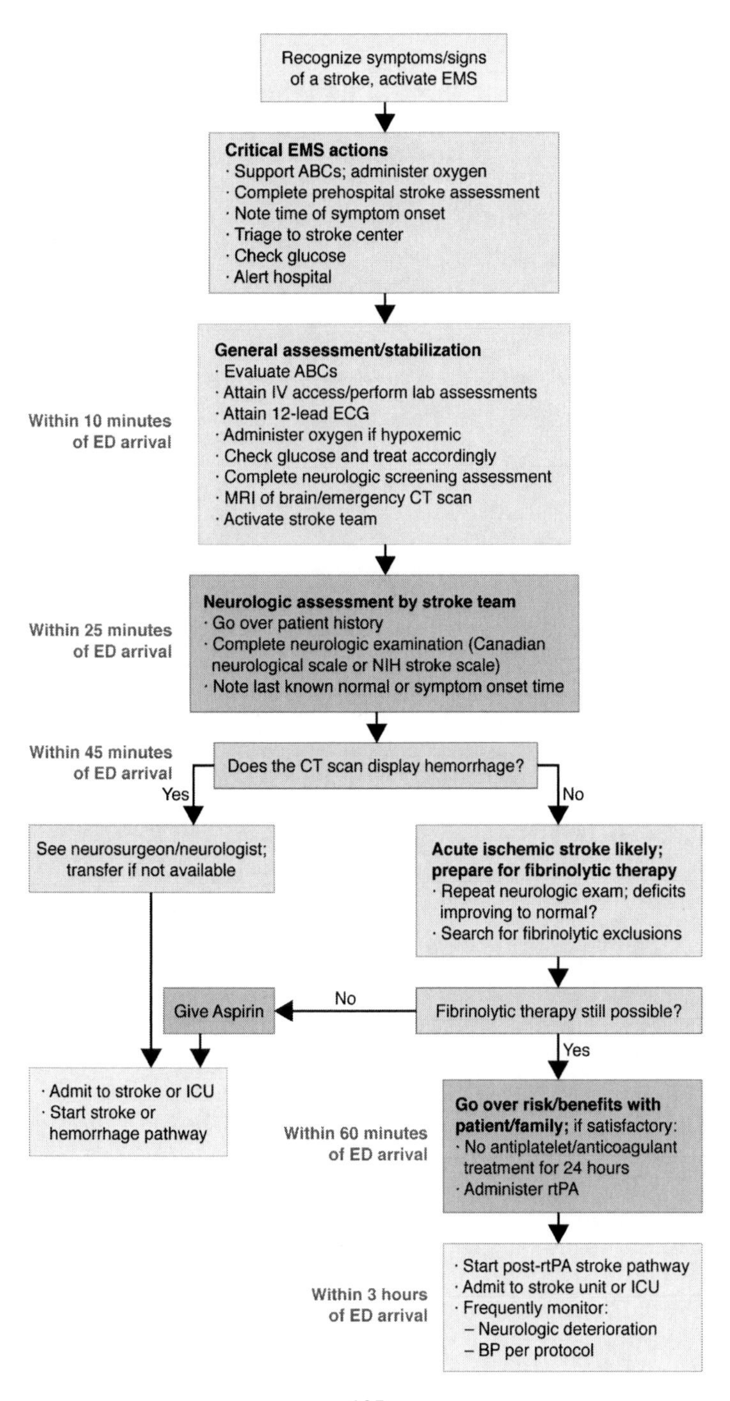

QUESTIONS

1. Which of the following conditions must be ruled out because it can mimic stroke?

   a. Hypokalemia
   b. Hypoglycemia
   c. Hyperthyroidism
   d. Hypothermia

2. What is the time frame within which a CT scan must be obtained and interpreted?

   a. 10 minutes
   b. 25 minutes
   c. 40 minutes
   d. 60 minutes

3. What drug may be given if fibrinolytic therapy is not possible?

   a. Heparin
   b. Aspirin
   c. Clopidogrel
   d. Warfarin

UNIT VII: ACLS CONSIDERATIONS IN SPECIAL POPULATIONS

CHAPTER 1

ACLS Considerations in Pediatric Patients

KEY 2020 GUIDELINE UPDATES

- If the infant/child has a pulse but inadequate respiration, provide 20 to 30 rescue breaths per minute or 1 breath every 2 to 3 seconds. The same rate is applicable when providing CPR with an advanced airway.
- For endotracheal intubation, cuffed ET tubes are preferred over uncuffed tubes. Routine use of cricoid pressure is not recommended during intubation.
- Epinephrine must be administered within 5 minutes of the start of chest compressions.
- CPR quality may be monitored using continuous invasive arterial pressure, if already in place.
- In the post-cardiac arrest period, evaluation should be carried out to detect seizures.
- Cardiac arrest survivors must be evaluated for rehabilitation services.

It must always be remembered that children are not miniature adults; this rule certainly applies to ACLS as well. It has been estimated that more than 20,000 pediatric patients suffer from cardiac arrest each year in the United States; less than half (7000) occur outside hospital, which implies that more importance needs to be given to prevention of cardiac arrest in pediatric patients.

For the purposes of ACLS, the AHA considers any patient below the age of 18 as a pediatric patient. All pediatric patients may be further categorized as:

- Neonates: Infants less than 30 days old
- Infants: Children below 1 year of age
- Children: Patients from one year of age till puberty.
- Adolescents: Patients are considered as adolescents if they exhibit secondary signs of puberty – breast development in female patients, and development of axillary hair in male patients. ACLS for adolescents may follow guidelines prescribed for adult patients.

The pediatric chain of survival, which is slightly different from the adult chain of survival, is presented below. It must be noted that, unlike adult patients, the first step in the out-of-hospital chain of survival is 'prevention of arrest', rather than calling for help. This is because unlike adults, children usually develop respiratory arrest prior to cardiac arrest. Immediate intervention can help prevent cardiac arrest, and help restore spontaneous breathing. If a cell phone is readily available, initiating CPR and calling for help may be done simultaneously. However, if cellphone access or help is not immediately available, the rescuer must initiate a cycle of CPR before attempting to call for help.

ALGORITHM 11: PEDIATRIC CHAIN OF SURVIVAL

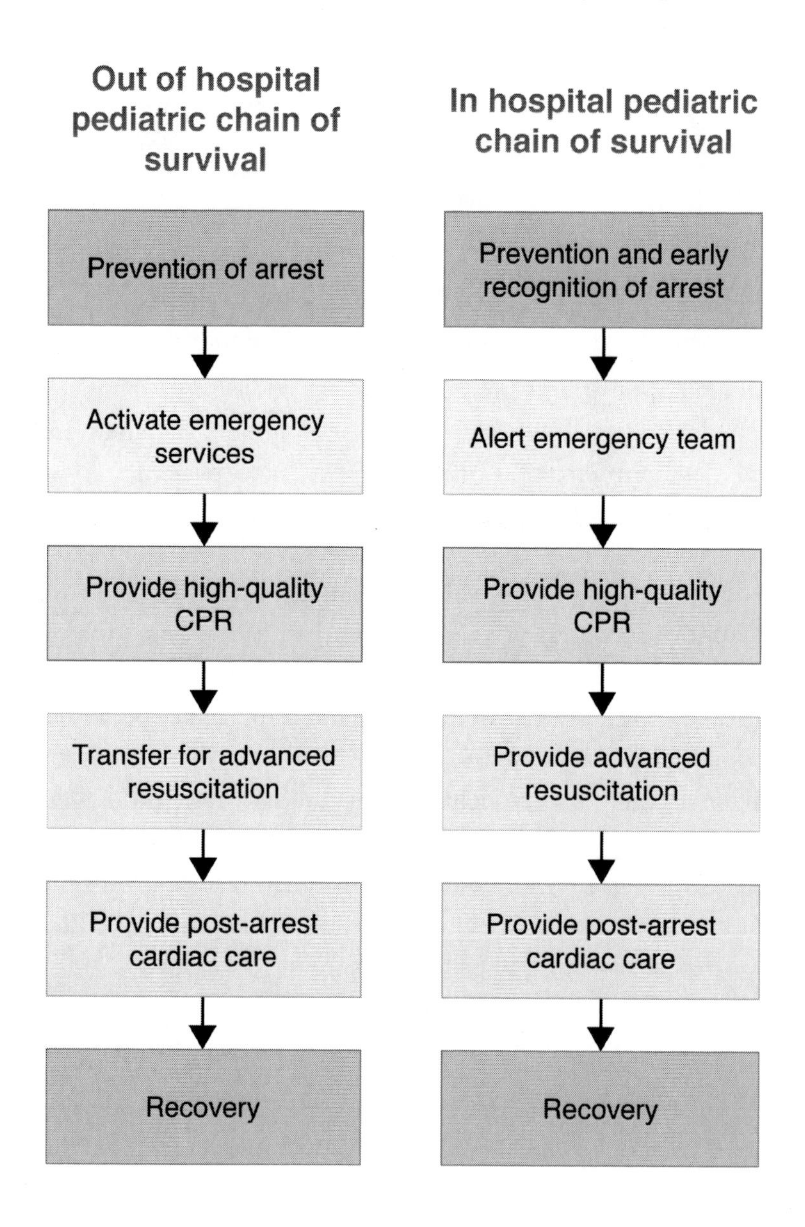

The ACLS algorithm to be followed in pediatric patients is described below. Specific differences are discussed following the algorithm.

ALGORITHM 12: PEDIATRIC ACLS ALGORITHM

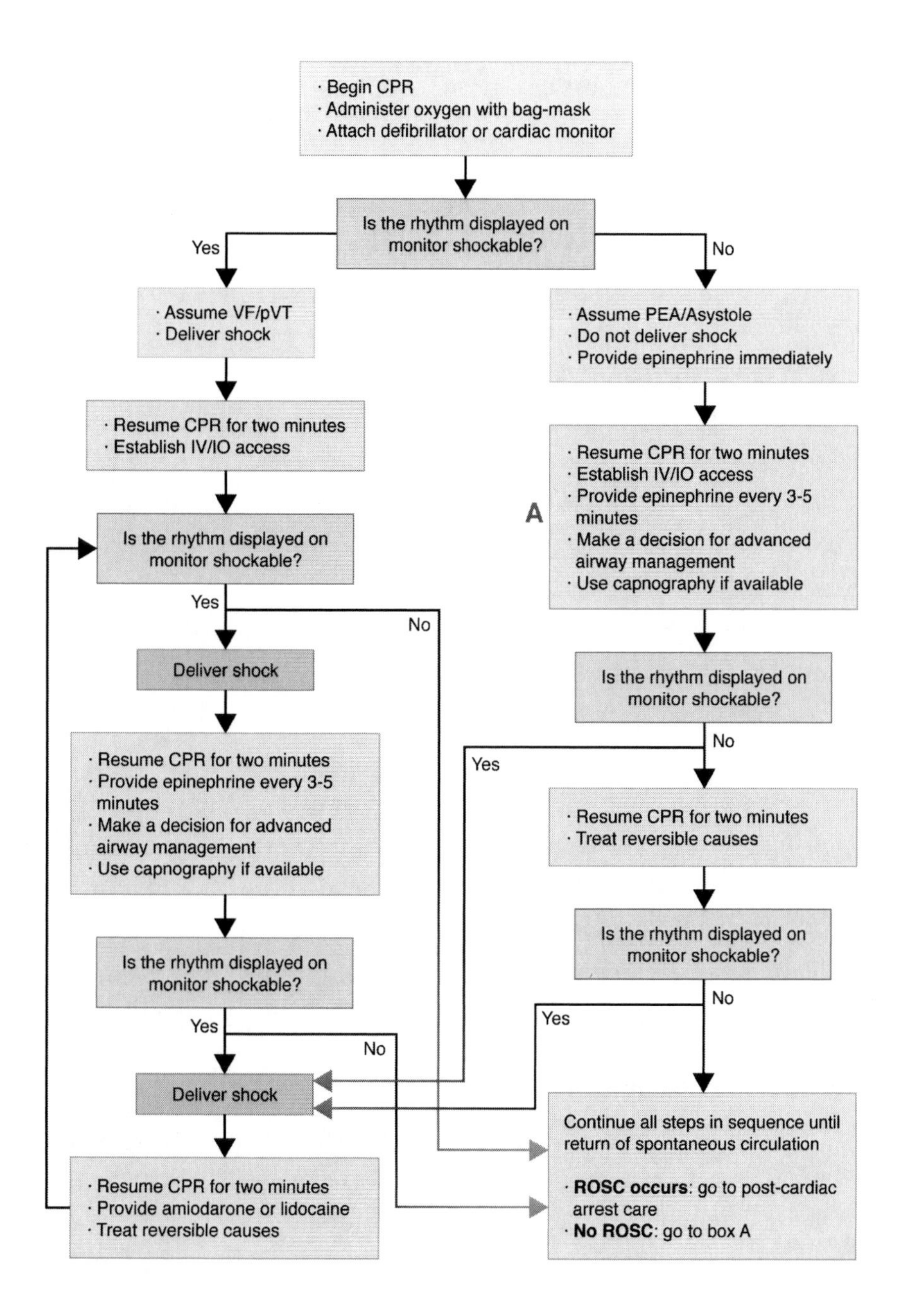

Chest Compressions:

The basic technique of CPR in pediatric patients remains the same. The AHA recommends following a C-A-B approach rather than an A-B-C approach to optimize circulation. Ideally, chest compressions must be combined with rescue breathing. However, if the rescuer is unable or unwilling to provide rescue breathing, at least chest compressions should be given.

For children:

- Chest compressions must be given at a rate of 100 to 120 per minute. The chest must be allowed to recoil completely after each compression. The depth of compression, however, differs from adults. The depth must ideally be one-third the antero-posterior diameter of the chest. This is usually 5cm (2 inches) in children, and 4 cm (1.5 inches) for infants.
- Every two minutes, a rhythm check may be performed, which must not last longer than 10 seconds.

For infants:

- Chest compressions must be performed by compressing the sternum using two fingers, or encircling the entire chest with the palms of both hands, and using both thumbs to compress the sternum just below the intermammary line.
- If the required depth is not achievable using the above technique, the heel of one hand may be used for compressions.

Airway and Ventilation:

- In the out-of-hospital setting, it may be reasonable to use bag-mask ventilation as opposed to advanced airway, as usage of both techniques has resulted in equivalent patient outcomes.
- When an advanced airway is not available, a compression: ventilation ratio of 30: 2 must be used if only a single rescuer is available. If

two rescuers are available, a compression: ventilation ratio of 15: 2 is recommended.

- 100% oxygen must be used for ventilation.
- If advanced airway is to be placed, a cuffed ET tube is preferred over an uncuffed tube. A tube of proper size and diameter must be chosen, and the cuff inflation pressure must be less than 20 to 25 cm H20.
- When an advanced airway is in place, one rescue breath may be used every 2 to 3 seconds, totaling 20 to 30 breaths per minute.

Drug administration:

- As with adults, usage of epinephrine is recommended as part of the ACLS protocol. Intravenous route or intraosseous routes are most preferred.
- Epinephrine must be administered within 5 minutes of beginning chest compressions, and must be delivered every 3 to 5 minutes until return of spontaneous circulation occurs.
- Amiodarone or lidocaine may be used for ventricular fibrillation or pulseless ventricular tachycardia that does not respond to shock.
- Sodium bicarbonate is not indicated, except in cases of hyperkalemia or tricyclic antidepressant toxicity.
- Calcium administration is not indicated, unless there is documented evidence of hyperkalemia, hypermagnesemia, hypocalcemia, or calcium channel blocker overdose.
- For all drugs that are administered, dosage must be calculated based on weight. However, these doses must not exceed the recommended adult dose. If weight is unknown, cognitive aids such as a body length tape may be used to aid in weight calculation.

Defibrillation:

Choosing a device:

- If an AED is used for children below 8 years of age, a model with a pediatric attenuator must be chosen if available.
- For infants, a manual defibrillator is preferable, particularly when a shockable rhythm has been identified.
- If the above defibrillator models are not available, using an AED without a pediatric attenuator is preferable to no defibrillation.

Choosing adhesive pads or paddles:

- Either pads or paddles may be used. The largest size that comfortably fits the child's chest without touching one another must be chosen.
- For self-adhesive pads, both antero-posterior and anterolateral placement are equally effective.

Energy doses:

- The initial dose of energy delivered must be 2 J/kg of body weight.
- For subsequent attempts, the energy dose may be increased to 4 J/kg and upwards. However, the dose must not exceed 10 J/kg.

Identifying known causes of arrest:

Echocardiography may be considered if it can be performed without interrupting or compromising the quality of chest compressions. This may help identify known causes of arrest, such as cardiac tamponade and compromised ventricular filling.

POST-CARDIAC ARREST CARE IN PEDIATRIC PATIENTS

Pediatric patients who recover from cardiac arrest are at risk of developing post-cardiac arrest syndrome. This syndrome may include the following components:

- Brain injury
- Myocardial dysfunction
- Systemic ischemia and reperfusion response
- Persistence of precipitating pathophysiology.

To manage this complex quartet, post-cardiac arrest care includes the following parameters:

Targeted temperature management:

- Maintaining the core temperature within a narrow prescribed range can help avoid fever. In addition, maintaining lower core temperatures would reduce the body's metabolic demand, which in turn would reduce free radical production and decrease apoptosis.
- If patients do not regain consciousness following ROSC, it is recommended that core temperatures be maintained between 32°C and 34°C for 48 hours, followed by temperatures between 36°C and 37.5°C for 3 days. Alternatively, only 36°C and 37.5°C may be maintained for 5 days.
- When rewarming the patient, it is important to continuously monitor blood pressure and treat hypotension promptly.

Post-cardiac arrest ventilation and oxygenation management:

- Oxygen saturation must be maintained between 94% and 99%.
- Monitoring partial pressure of carbondioxide is essential to prevent patients from going into hypocapnea or hypercapnea.
- The patient's underlying condition must always be taken into account while determining optimal PaO2 and PaCO2 levels.

Hemodynamic monitoring:

- Cardiac telemetry may be used to monitor the patient's vital signs remotely. Arterial blood pressure must be continuously monitored.
- Systolic blood pressure must be maintained above the fifth percentile for the particular age and gender. If necessary, fluid boluses and inotropic drugs or vasopressors must be used to achieve this goal.
- Continuous monitoring of central venous oxygen saturation, urine output, and serum lactate levels can guide circulatory therapies.
- Serum blood glucose and electrolytes must be frequently monitored and corrected to achieve optimal levels.

Neurological assessment:

- Continuous EEG monitoring in order to identify and manage seizures.
- Any clinical seizures, and nonclinical status epilepticus must be treated, in consultation with neurological experts.

Prognostication in pediatric patients

- There are currently no reliable factors or algorithms to guide prognostication in pediatric patients. Experts believe that a number of factors must be considered, including clinical history, elevated serum lactate, and high pH.
- EEG patterns have emerged as an important prognosticator. A normal background, sleep spindles, and reactivity are associated with favorable outcomes, while flat, attenuated EEG patterns, and burst suppression are associated with poor outcomes. However, other factors apart from EEG must be taken into account while considering a prognosis.

QUESTIONS

1. During chest compressions, what depth of compression must be maintained for infants?

   a. 1 inch
   b. 1.5 inches
   c. 2 inches
   d. 2.5 inches

2. For pediatric defibrillation, what is the initial energy dose to be delivered?

   a. 1 J/kg
   b. 2 J/kg
   c. 4 J/kg
   d. 6 J/kg

3. Which of the following EEG patterns are associated with poor neurological outcome?

   a. Sleep spindles
   b. Reactivity
   c. Normal background
   d. Burst suppression

CHAPTER 2

Addressing Specific Pediatric Clinical Situations

Most cases of pediatric cardiac arrest, barring traumatic cardiac arrest, occur when the patient has an underlying medical condition. When these conditions are present, it may be prudent to manage them appropriately to prevent arrest. Some medical conditions that can lead to cardiac arrest are discussed below.

MANAGEMENT OF SHOCK

Shock is defined as a state of complete circulatory collapse because there is a failure of oxygen to meet the metabolic demands of the body. The most common type of shock that occurs in pediatric patients is hypovolemic or hemorrhagic shock. Cardiogenic shock and septic shock are less frequent. Regardless of the etiology, fluid administration remains the mainstay of management in shock patients. The following recommendations are made for the management of shock in pediatric patients:

General recommendations:

- After each bolus of fluid administration, the patient must be reassessed both for responsiveness and for signs of fluid overload.
- The initial fluid of choice may either be crystalloids or colloids, and either balanced or unbalanced solutions. For patients with hemorrhagic shock, however, administration of blood products may be considered rather than crystalloids or colloids.

Recommendations for septic shock:

- For pediatric patients with septic shock, IV fluids may be administered in 10ml/kg or 20ml/kg aliquots with frequent reassessment.
- If the septic shock is fluid-refractory, a vasoactive infusion of either epinephrine or norepinephrine may be given. If both are unavailable, dopamine may be considered.
- For pediatric patients in whom fluids are unresponsive and vasoactive support is needed, stress-dose corticosteroids may be considered.

Recommendations for cardiogenic shock:

- Early expert consultation must be obtained.
- An inotropic infusion of epinephrine, dopamine, dobutamine, or milrinone may be considered.

MANAGEMENT OF RESPIRATORY FAILURE:

Respiratory failure consists of ineffective oxygenation and ventilation, which could occur due to several causes. The leading causes of respiratory failure include foreign body airway obstruction and opioid overdose.

General management of inadequate breathing when a pulse is present:

- If there is absent or inadequate respiratory effort, rescue breathing must be provided immediately.
- Ideally, one rescue breath must be provided every 2 to 3 seconds, totaling 20 to 30 breaths per minute.
- If emergency intubation is to be performed, the patient may be at risk of developing bradycardia. To prevent this, atropine (0.02 mg/kg) may be used as premedication.

Management of foreign body airway obstruction:

- In mild cases where the child is conscious, the child must be encouraged to clear the airway by coughing.

- In cases of severe airway obstruction, the Heimlich maneuver must be attempted for children, in the form of abdominal thrusts, until the object is expelled or the child becomes unresponsive.
- For infants with severe airway obstruction, a continuous cycle of five back blows followed by five chest compressions must be performed, until the object is expelled or the infant becomes unresponsive.
- If the patient becomes unresponsive, begin CPR immediately, and follow the ACLS algorithm described in the previous chapter.
- When the airway is opened during CPR, remove any foreign object present if it is visible. Under no circumstances must a blind finger sweep be performed, as this carries the risk of pushing the object deeper into the airway.

Management of a child with suspected opioid overdose:

- For pediatric patients with suspected opioid overdose, bag-mask ventilation must be maintained till spontaneous breathing returns; else pediatric ACLS protocols must be followed. It is reasonable for rescuers to administer intramuscular or intranasal naloxone.
- The ACLS algorithm described for management of opioid overdose in adults must be followed.

MANAGEMENT OF PEDIATRIC BRADYCARDIA:

- In pediatric patients who develop bradycardia, an effort must be made to ascertain and address the cause, while simultaneously monitoring the airway and ventilation.
- If the oxygenation and ventilation is effective, but bradycardia persists, CPR must begin immediately.
- If the cause of bradycardia is increased vagal tone, or primary atrioventricular conduction block, atropine may be administered.
- If bradycardia persists after correction of the cause, epinephrine may be given through IV or IO route.

- If the cause of bradycardia is complete heart block or sinoatrial node dysfunction, and it is unresponsive to ventilation, CPR, and medication, emergency transcutaneous pacing may be performed.

The comprehensive management of pediatric bradycardia is outlined in the algorithm below.

ALGORITHM 13: PEDIATRIC BRADYCARDIA HAVING A PULSE ACLS

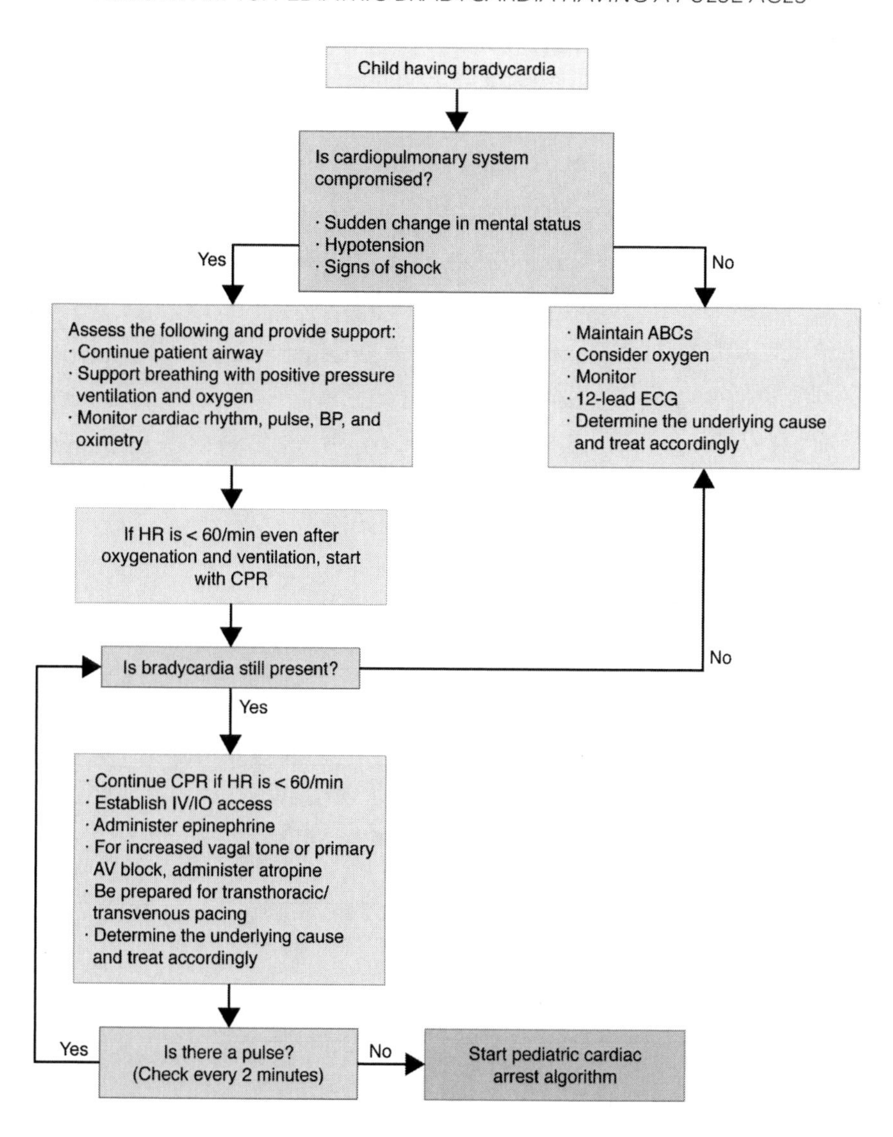

MANAGEMENT OF PEDIATRIC TACHYCARDIA:

- The management of pediatric tachycardia, like the management for adult patients, would depend on the kind of abnormal rhythm that is present.

Management of supraventricular tachycardia, when pulse is present:

- If the patient is hemodynamically unstable, and there is evidence of cardiovascular compromise (signs of hypotension, shock, or altered mental status), electric synchronized cardioversion must be performed. Initially, a dose of 0.5 J to 1 J/kg must be used, and this may be increased to 2 J/kg if unsuccessful.
- In hemodynamically stable patients, SVT should ideally be treated with adenosine, administered through IV or IO route. Vagal stimulation may also be attempted.
- If the patient is unresponsive to both adenosine and vagal stimulation, expert consultation must be obtained.
- If expert consultation is not available, administration of procainamide or amiodarone may be considered.

Management of wide complex tachycardia:

- If the patient is hemodynamically stable, expert consultation must first be obtained.
- If the patient is hemodynamically unstable, and there is evidence of cardiovascular compromise, electric synchronized cardioversion must be performed. Initially, a dose of 0.5 J to 1 J/kg must be used, and this may be increased to 2 J/kg if unsuccessful.

A comprehensive algorithm for the management of tachycardia in pediatric patients is outlined below.

ALGORITHM 14: MANAGEMENT OF PEDIATRIC TACHYCARDIA

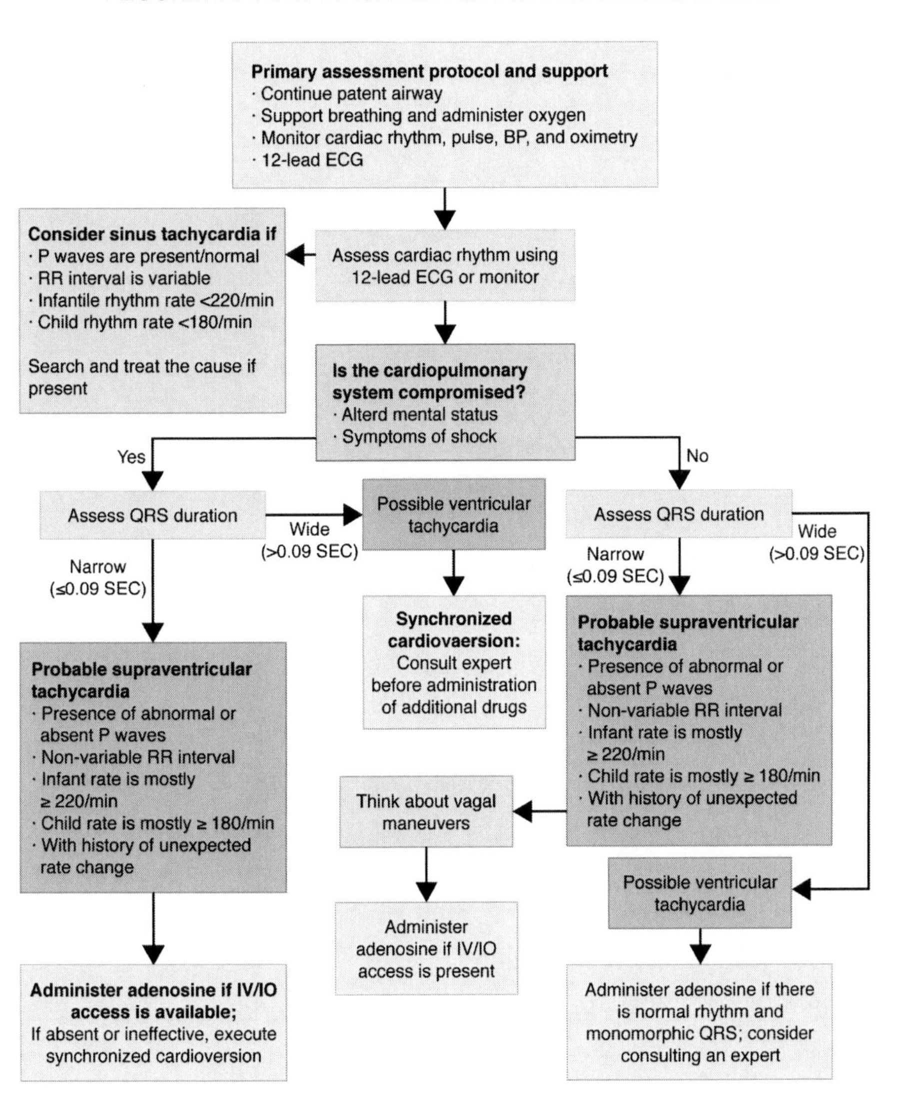

MANAGEMENT OF PATIENTS WITH MYOCARDITIS AND CARDIOMYOPATHY:

Myocarditis refers to inflammation of the cardiac muscle, which can lead to a decrease in cardiac output and cause hypoxia to end organs. Cardiomyopathy can also decrease cardiac efficiency and lead to decompensated heart failure. The following are the AHA recommendations for the management of such patients:

- Patients with myocarditis are at high risk of cardiac arrest and must therefore be transferred to the ICU for advanced management.
- Extracorporeal life support, or mechanical circulatory support may be beneficial for these patients to prevent cardiac arrest and provide end-organ circulatory support.
- Due to compromised cardiac muscle, conventional ACLS support may be challenging in these patients. Therefore, if cardiac arrest occurs, extracorporeal resuscitation may be beneficial.

MANAGEMENT OF PATIENTS WITH A SINGLE VENTRICLE:

Single ventricle disease, refers to a number of congenital conditions in which either one of the ventricles is underdeveloped and may be non-functional. Patients born with such conditions may need to undergo a series of staged surgical procedures with the following goals:

- To provide unobstructed systemic blood circulation
- To allow effective atrial communications
- To optimize pulmonary blood flow so that volume load on the left ventricle is minimized

Due to imbalances in pulmonary and systemic blood flow, and increased myocardial work, such patients are always at increased risk of cardiac arrest. The management of cardiac arrest will depend on the stage of surgical procedure that the patient is at.

Prior to Stage I repair:

- In neonates, before Stage I repair, a target PaCO2 of 50 to 60 mmHg must be achieved, either by mechanical ventilation, or through appropriate analgesia and sedation.

Patient who have undergone Stage I procedures:

- Oxygen saturation must be constantly monitored.
- Systemic vascular resistance may be lowered using alpha-adrenergic inhibitors, or phosphodiesterase III inhibitors.
- Extracorporeal life support may increase systemic oxygen delivery.
- If there is obstruction of the surgically placed shunt, it is reasonable to administer oxygen, vasoactive agents, and heparin (50 to 100 units/kg bolus).

Patients who have undergone Stage II repair:

- Maintenance of mild respiratory acidosis and a minimum mean airway pressure can improve cerebral and systemic arterial oxygenation.
- If systemic oxygen delivery is low, extracorporeal life support may be considered.

MANAGEMENT OF PATIENTS WITH PULMONARY HYPERTENSION:

In pediatric patients, pulmonary hypertension may either be idiopathic, or secondary to lung or heart disease. This condition can lead to elevated ventricular pressure, leading to a fall in left heart filling and cardiac output. Pulmonary hypertensive crises can lead to cardiac arrest if not handled immediately.

- During pulmonary hypertensive crises, initial therapy should consist of prostacyclin or inhaled nitric oxide.
- Respiratory function must be monitored carefully to avoid hypoxia and acidosis.

- Alkalosis may be induced by administering alkali or through hyperventilation.
- If patients are known to be at high risk of developing pulmonary hypertensive crises, they may be treated with analgesics, sedatives, and neuromuscular blocking agents.
- Extracorporeal life support may be considered for those patients who develop respiratory failure and low cardiac output, and fail to respond to medical therapy.

QUESTIONS

1. What is the fluid of choice to be given in hemorrhagic shock?
   a. Saline
   b. Ringer's lactate
   c. Colloids
   d. Blood

2. What is the first drug of choice in pediatric bradycardia due to primary AV block?
   a. Epinephrine
   b. Atropine
   c. Adenosine
   d. Lignocaine

3. Do electric cardioversion in pediatric patients, what is the initial energy level that must be selected?
   a. 0.5 to 1 J/kg
   b. 1 to 1.5 J/kg
   c. 1.5 to 2 J/kg
   d. 2 to 2.5 J/kg

CHAPTER 3

Neonatal Life Support

It is estimated that for every 10 births, at least 1 neonate needs some form of life support. Providing such support will require a dedicated one-on-one approach, from a trained caregiver. All medical facilities must have resources on hand to provide neonatal life support. In their 2020 guidelines, the AHA has introduced a specific neonatal resuscitation algorithm.

Initial actions after birth:

- Majority of newborn infants do not require immediate cord clamping or resuscitation. Prevention of hypothermia is the primary focus after birth. The infant baby must be dried, and directly placed for skin-to-skin contact with the mother, maintaining a warm temperature. The initial evaluation can then be performed prior to cord clamping.
- The baby must be evaluated for normal respiratory transition. If necessary, the baby may be stimulated for respiratory effort. The airway may be examined and cleared using suction if required.
- Even if resuscitation is not required, skin-to-skin contact can improve temperature control, blood glucose stability, and breastfeeding abilities.
- If further resuscitation efforts are required, it may be appropriate to perform them with temperature controlling measures in place. This could involve increased room temperature, use of radiant warmers,

and even plastic bags or caps. Exothermic mattresses are effective in preventing hypothermia.

Heart rate:

This may be assessed by auscultation or palpation.

Positive pressure ventilation:

- If the infant is apneic, or has a low heart rate, positive pressure ventilation must be provided. This alone is effective in most infants. A rise in the heart rate, or evidence of breathing and/or crying is indicative of effective ventilation and successful resuscitation.
- Initially, positive pressure ventilation may be initiated with 21% oxygen for term infants and 21% to 30% oxygen for preterm infants. Monitor oxygen saturation levels using pulse oximetry. A peak inflation pressure of 20 to 25 mmH20 must be used; excessive inflation pressures can be harmful.
- If there is evidence of airway obstruction during PPV, endotracheal intubation and tracheal suctioning may be beneficial. However, routine laryngoscopy and endotracheal suctioning is not recommended.
- If the infant is breathing spontaneously, but still requires respiratory support, it may be reasonable to use continuous positive airway pressure (CPAP) rather than intubation.

Chest compressions:

- Positive pressure ventilation should not last more than 30 seconds. After this, if the heart rate remains below 60 beats per minute, chest compressions should be initiated.
- The two thumb-encircling hands technique is preferred for chest compressions. Three compressions must be followed by an inflation (90 compressions and 30 inflations per minute).
- Response to chest compressions may be monitored using an ECG.

Systemic access:

- For newborn infants, the umbilical vein may provide the best route of access. Intraosseous access may be considered if this is unsuccessful.
- Administer epinephrine and/or volume expanders in neonates who fail to respond to chest compressions and PPV.
- If there is no response to the initial resuscitative measures, and blood loss is either known or suspected, volume expansion with normal saline (0.9% sodium chloride) or blood at 10 to 20 mL/kg may be considered.

The comprehensive algorithm for management of the neonate immediately after birth is detailed below.

ALGORITHM 15: NEONATAL RESUSCITATION ALGORITHM

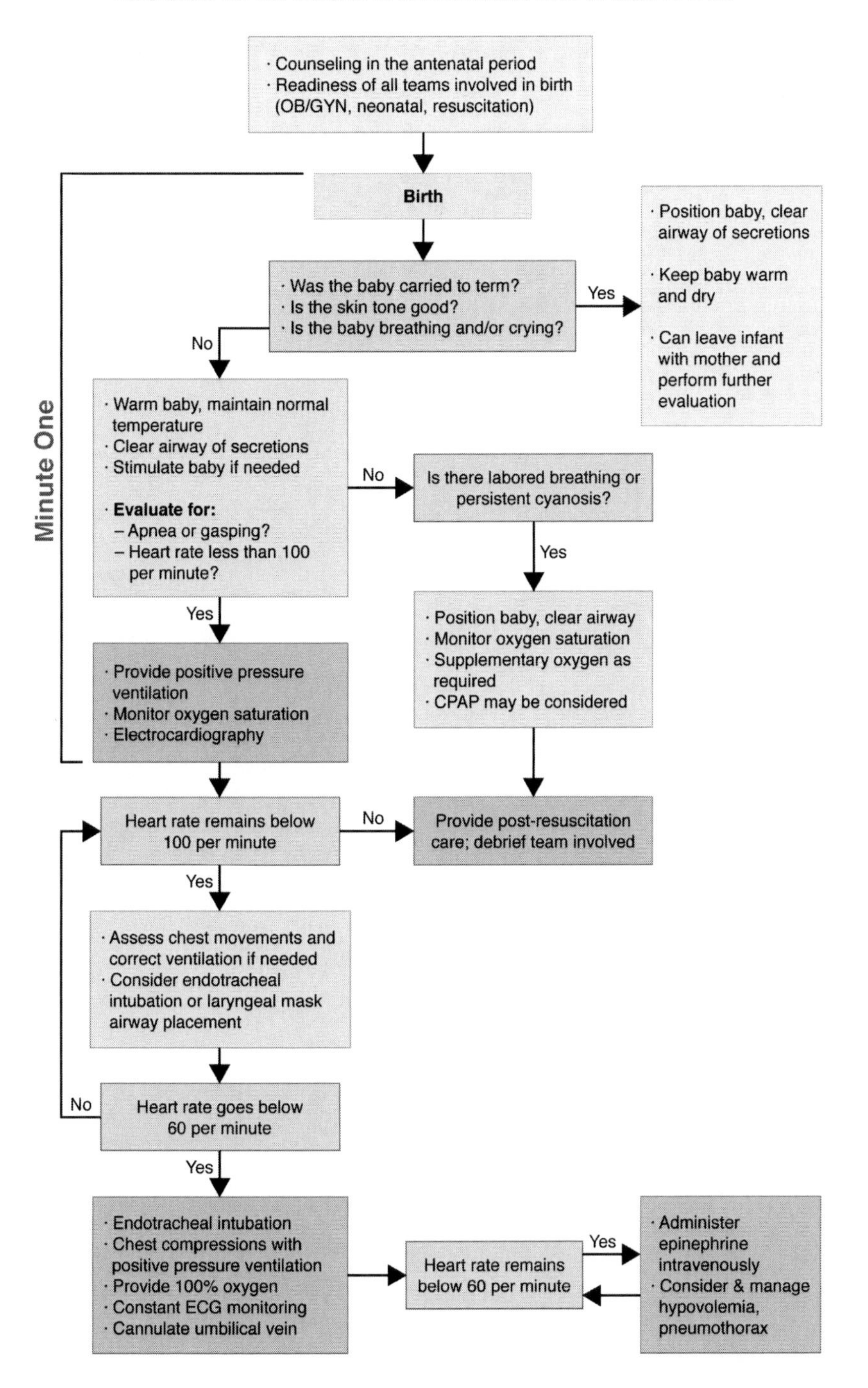

Termination of resuscitation efforts:

If all the steps in the above algorithm have been followed, and there is no response at the end of 20 minutes, it may be reasonable to discuss cessation of resuscitation efforts with the family. The likelihood of survival is extremely low if the newborn has failed to respond for over 20 minutes.

QUESTIONS

1. Immediately after delivery, what is the most important step that must be carried out for healthy neonates who do not require resuscitation?
   a. Maternal skin-to-skin contact
   b. Cord clamping
   c. Stimulation of breathing
   d. Delivery of afterbirth

2. What is the rate of chest compressions to be given for neonatal life support?
   a. 30 per minute
   b. 60 per minute
   c. 90 per minute
   d. 120 per minute

3. When should termination of resuscitative efforts be considered for neonates?
   a. 10 minutes
   b. 20 minutes
   c. 30 minutes
   d. 40 minutes

CHAPTER 4

ACLS Considerations in Pregnant Patients

KEY 2020 GUIDELINE UPDATES

- If cardiac arrest occurs during pregnancy, focus must remain on maternal resuscitation. Fetal monitoring must not be undertaken as it can interfere with resuscitation.
- Oxygen and airway management must be prioritized as these patients are more prone to hypoxia.
- Targeted temperature management is recommended for comatose patients post-cardiac arrest, but with continuous fetal monitoring to avoid bradycardia.

Pregnant patients deserve special consideration because two lives may be impacted if a pregnant woman goes into cardiac arrest. Making a decision to prioritize a mother's life over the fetus, or vice-versa, may be a difficult one, and is best made based on literature evidence. Literature evidence shows that the best chances for both maternal and fetal survival are obtained through successful maternal resuscitation.

The AHA states that the incidence of maternal cardiac arrest during delivery is rare, but appears to be increasing. The various causes of maternal cardiac arrest during delivery include:

- Cardiac failure
- Hemorrhage
- Amniotic fluid embolism
- Aspiration pneumonitis
- Sepsis
- Venous thromboembolism
- Pre-eclampsia or eclampsia
- Complications from anesthesia

Management of cardiac arrest in pregnancy:

Ideally, definitive management should include a skilled team of specialists, including an obstetrician, neonatologist, emergency room physician, anesthesiologist, and intensivist. The complete resuscitation team must also be on hand.

Special considerations for CPR in pregnancy:

- Manual displacement of the uterus must be performed to the left side, prior to delivering chest compressions. This will provide relief from aortocaval compression, and will improve venous return and cardiac output. Initially, left lateral uterine displacement may be performed with both hands. During CPR, one-handed displacement must be done to avoid interference with compressions.
- Pregnant patients are more prone to hypoxia as compared to normal adults. Therefore, airway management and oxygenation must take high priority.
- Obtaining a patent airway in a pregnant patient can be challenging. Therefore, the first attempt must be made by experienced providers. If possible, endotracheal intubation or supraglottic advanced airways are preferable.
- After advanced airway placement, deliver one rescue breath every 6 seconds (10 breaths per minute), while performing continuous chest compressions.

- Fetal monitoring must not be undertaken during the maternal resuscitation process, as this has the potential to interfere with the resuscitation process.

Recommendations and timing of perimortem cesarean delivery (PMCD):

PMCD is also referred to as resuscitative hysterectomy. Studies have shown that PMCD may improve fetal outcomes if undertaken when the fetus is greater than 20 weeks of age. Since it will not be immediately known if ROSC would occur, the perimortem team must be summoned if it is recognized that the patient appears to be in the second half of their pregnancy. The team should remain on standby till needed.

- To assess the age of the fetus, the position of the fundus may be used as a guide. If this is at or above the umbilicus, the patient may be assumed to be in the latter half of pregnancy.
- If ROSC does not occur after the usual resuscitation protocol, prepare for evacuation of the fetus while resuscitation continues.
- In certain situations, it may be immediately obvious that resuscitation efforts would be futile; such as nonsurvivable maternal trauma, or prolonged period of pulselessness. In such situations, PMCD need not be delayed.
- Ideally, PMCD should be performed within five minutes of cardiac arrest.

ALGORITHM 16: CARDIAC ARREST ACLS FOR PREGNANT WOMEN

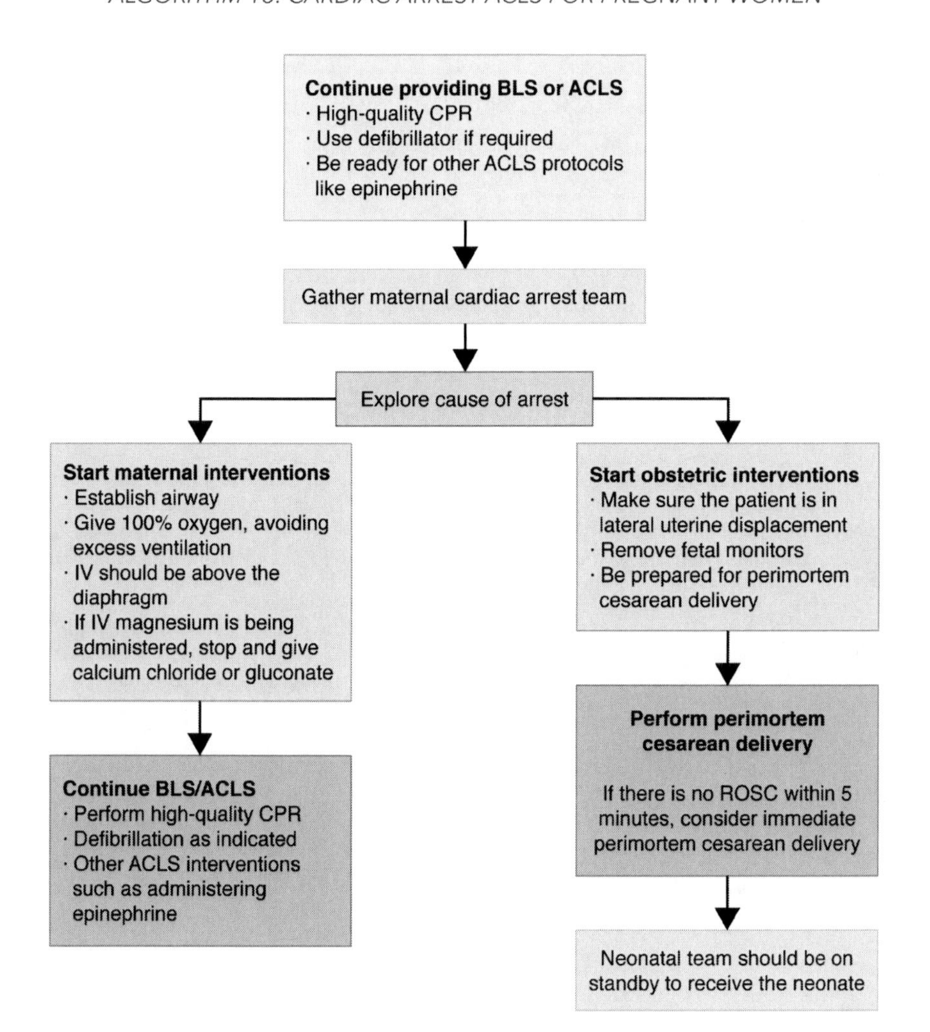

Post-cardiac arrest care in the pregnant patient:

- As with normal patients, targeted temperature management may be undertaken for pregnant patients who remain comatose after ROSC.
- However, during TTM, there must be continuous fetal monitoring, as fetal bradycardia is an extremely common complication. If this occurs, both obstetric and neonatal consultation must be obtained.

QUESTIONS

1. Which of the following parameters must be prioritized during ACLS support for the pregnant patient?
   a. Airway management
   b. Chest compressions
   c. Fetal monitoring
   d. Cesarean delivery of the fetus

2. How soon after cardiac arrest should perimortem cesarean delivery be performed?
   a. 5 minutes
   b. 10 minutes
   c. 15 minutes
   d. 20 minutes

3. During targeted temperature management of the post-arrest pregnant patient, what possible complication may be anticipated?
   a. Bradycardia
   b. Tachycardia
   c. Fetal bradycardia
   d. Fetal tachycardia

CHAPTER 5

ACLS Considerations in Patients with Known or Suspected Covid-19 Infection

Over the past year, the Covid-19 pandemic has necessitated shift in healthcare policies on a large scale; this also affects ACLS guidelines. On one hand, at least 12-19% of patients infected with the novel coronavirus require hospital admission; 3 to 6% become critically ill and are at risk of developing hypoxemic respiratory failure, which may go into cardiac arrest. On the other hand, the highly contagious nature of the virus, particularly novel strains, puts the ACLS provider at risk.

In April 2020, the AHA released an interim guidance for ACLS in patients with known or suspected Covid-19 infection. The following alterations were emphasized:

- Provider exposure to Covid-19 must be limited: Use personal protective equipment (PPE), limit personnel, use mechanical CPR devices.
- Prioritization of oxygenation and ventilation, while reducing aerosolization.
- Consider appropriateness of starting and continuing resuscitation.

ALGORITHM 17: ACLS ALGORITHM FOR PATIENTS WITH SUSPECTED OR CONFIRMED COVID-19

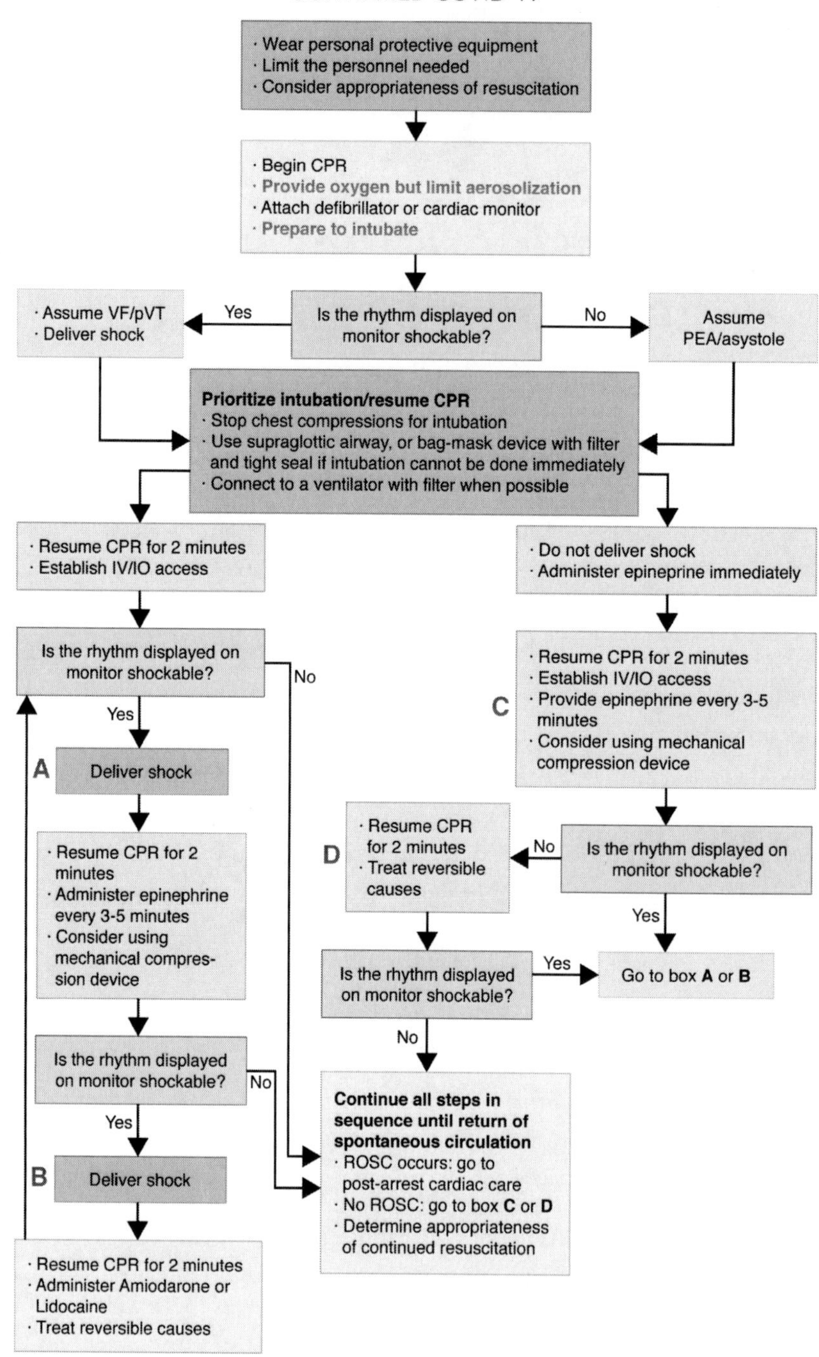

Answers to Exercises

UNIT II

1. B
2. A
3. D

UNIT III

1. D
2. C
3. B

UNIT IV

CHAPTER 2

1. B
2. A
3. B
4. C

CHAPTER 3

1. C
2. B
3. A

CHAPTER 4

1. C
2. D
3. C
4. D

CHAPTER 5

1. C
2. B
3. D

CHAPTER 6

1. B
2. B
3. B

UNIT V

1. A
2. C
3. B

UNIT VI

CHAPTER 1

1. D
2. C
3. D
4. D

CHAPTER 2

1. B
2. C

CHAPTER 3

1. B
2. C

CHAPTER 4

1. B
2. B
3. B

UNIT VII

CHAPTER 1

1. B
2. B
3. D

CHAPTER 2

1. D
2. B
3. A

CHAPTER 3

1. A
2. C
3. B

CHAPTER 4

1. A
2. A
3. C

Index

A

B

C

D

O

P

R

S

T

V

JOIN OUR COMMUNITY

Medical Creations® is an educational company focused on providing study tools for Healthcare students.

You can find all of our products at this link:

www.medicalcreations.net

If you have any questions or concerns please contact us:

hello@medicalcreations.net

We want to be as close as possible to our customers, that's why we are active on all the main Social Media platforms.

You can find us here:

Facebook	www.facebook.com/medicalcreations
Instagram	www.instagram.com/medicalcreationsofficial
Pinterest	www.pinterest.com/medicalcreations

CHECK OUT OUR OTHER BOOKS

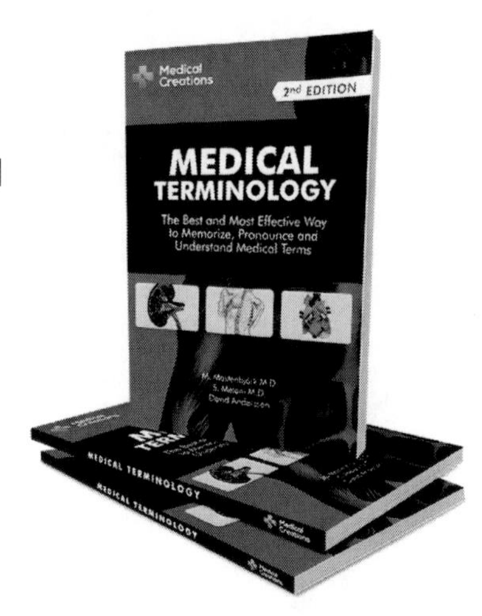

BEST SELLER ON AMAZON

MEDICAL TERMINOLOGY

The Best and Most Effective Way to Memorize, Pronounce and Understand Medical Terms (2nd Edition)

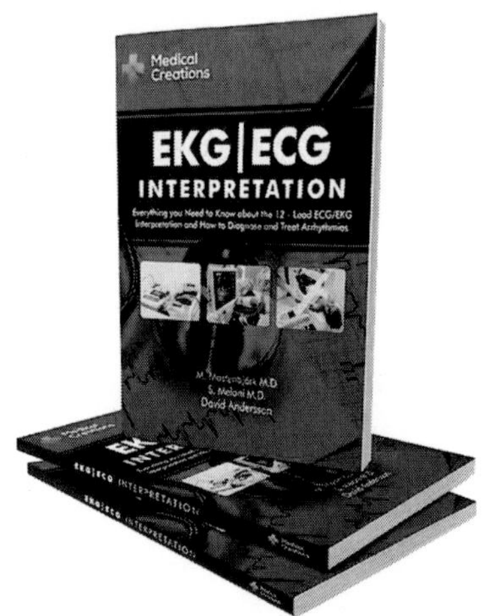

BEST SELLER ON AMAZON

EKG/ECG INTERPRETATION

Everything you Need to Know about the 12-Lead ECG/EKG Interpretation and How to Diagnose and Treat Arrhythmias

LAB VALUES

Everything You Need to Know about Laboratory Medicine and its Importance in the Diagnosis of Diseases

Made in United States
North Haven, CT
29 August 2023

40645168R00087